# AN INTRODUCTION TO
# THE PHILOSOPHY OF SRI AUROBINDO

S. K. MAITRA

*The late Head of the Department of Philosophy and Dean of the Faculty of Arts, Benares Hindu University*

SRI AUROBINDO ASHRAM
PONDICHERRY

First Edition: 1941
Second Edition: 1965
Sixth Impression: 2001

Rs. 15.00

ISBN 81-7058-346-2


Published by Sri Aurobindo Ashram Publication Department
Printed at Sri Aurobindo Ashram Press, Pondicherry

PRINTED IN INDIA

## PREFACE TO THE FIRST EDITION

When the last of the three articles which I wrote for the *Prabuddha Bharata* on *The Philosophy of Sri Aurobindo* appeared in the June number of that magazine, it occurred to me that these articles, if reprinted in book form with some additions and alterations, might serve the purpose of a short introduction to Sri Aurobindo's philosophy, which might be of some use to the public, as his great book *The Life Divine* was a voluminous work which many people could not find time to read. I therefore wrote to Swami Vipulanandaji, editor of the *Prabuddha Bharata*, for permission to reprint my articles in book forms. With the politeness and courtesy characteristic of the Swamijis of the Ramakrishna Mission, who have so worthily maintained the noble ideals of their great founder, he immediately replied, giving me his permission. I take this opportunity of thanking him for this act of kindness, without which this book would never have seen the light of the day.

The first three chapters of this book are practically a reprint, with slight changes, of the three articles which appeared in the *Prabuddha Bharata*. The fourth chapter is an altogether new one which I felt it necessary to add, as the account of Evolution given in the three articles in the *Prabuddha Bharata* was extremely meagre. An account of the nature of the Gnostic Being and the Divine Life I at first intended to include in the chapter on Evolution, but as that chapter had already grown too big, I ultimately decided to devote a separate chapter to it. And then I added a few concluding remarks by way of summing up the whole work.

## PREFACE

The account of Sri Aurobindo's philosophy which is presented in this book is mainly drawn from his great work *The Life Divine*. But I have also made use of his other works, such as his *Essays on the Gita*, *The Mother*, *Lights on Yoga* and *The Riddle of this World*. There is one topic which I have included in this *Introduction* which has not been mentioned in *The Life Divine* but has been dealt with very fully in *Essays on the Gita*—I mean the doctrine of Avatara which is one of the cardinal principles of the Bhagavad-Gita.

The book, as its title indicates, does not claim to be anything more than an introduction to Sri Aurobindo's philosophy. If it succeeds in creating in its readers an interest in his philosophy, so as to lead them to read the books of Sri Aurobindo himself, I shall feel that my labour has not been in vain.

S. K. *MAITRA*

Benares Hindu University,
*the 15th September, 1941*

# CONTENTS


| | | |
|---|---|---|
| I. | General Principles ... ... ... | 1 |
| II. | The Supermind and The Psychic Being ... | 16 |
| III. | The Descent or Involution ... ... | 32 |
| IV. | The Ascent or Evolution ... ... | 43 |
| V. | The Gnostic Being and The Divine Life ... | 56 |
| | Conclusion ... ... ... ... | 68 |

## CHAPTER I

# GENERAL PRINCIPLES

### *Philosophy must steer clear of Two Negations*

The fundamental idea upon which the whole structure of Sri Aurobindo's philosophy rests is that Matter as well as Spirit is to be looked upon as real. It will not do therefore for philosophy to ignore Matter as it will not do for it to ignore Spirit. A spiritualistic philosophy that totally negates Matter is as one-sided as a materialistic philosophy that totally ignores Spirit. The two extremes, therefore, which philosophy must avoid are materialism ignoring Spirit and spiritualism ignoring Matter.

For this reason Sri Aurobindo declares, "The affirmation of a divine life upon earth and an immortal sense in mortal existence can have no base unless we recognize not only eternal Spirit as the inhabitant of the bodily mansion, the wearer of this mutable robe, but accept Matter of which it is made as a fit and noble material out of which He weaves constantly His garbs, builds recurrently the unending series of His mansions" (*The Life Divine*, p. 8). We must say with our ancient forefathers, "Matter also is Brahman" (*annam brahmeti vyajānāt*). The inevitable result of separating Matter from Spirit is, as Sri Aurobindo points out, to force us to make a choice between the two. This is, in fact, what we actually notice in the history of human thought. Either Spirit has been denied as an illusion of the imagination or Matter has been denied as an illusion of the senses. The result is either "a great bankruptcy of Life" or "an equal bankruptcy in the things of the Spirit."

The materialist's denial of the Spirit rests upon an apotheosis of sensuous knowledge. The senses are for the materialist the sole means of knowledge. Reason, if it goes in any way beyond the data of the senses, must be pronounced to be a false guide.

The extreme narrowness of the materialist's position is its own undoing. There is no possibility of denying the creative function of the mind and the still higher powers of the Spirit in the shaping of our knowledge. There are vast fields which are inaccessible to the senses. And even in the regions where the senses function, the knowledge that is obtained is not tied down to the senses. All knowledge, *qua* knowledge, exhibits a transcendence of the senses, a reconstruction of the sensuous material by the mind and the higher powers of the Spirit.

But materialism, formidable as it was in the eighteenth and nineteenth centuries, is now greatly discredited and is no longer such an obstacle to the understanding of the true nature of Reality as the other one-sided theory, the spiritualism which denies altogether the reality of the sensuous world. The spiritualistic negation of the physical world is called by Sri Aurobindo "The Refusal of the Ascetic", and is pronounced by him to be "more complete, more final, more perilous in its effects on individuals or collectivities that hear its potent call to the wilderness" than the materialistic denial of the spiritual world.

This one-sided affirmation of the Spirit is the characteristic note of Indian thought as we find it in the Vedanta. Due to the predominant position which the Vedanta occupies in our country, this way of thinking even now dominates Indian thought, which is still more or less under the shadow of "the great Refusal," as Sri Aurobindo calls it.

Not that this line of thought has not been of help in the development of our culture. It has done tremendous service in quickening the spiritual life. It has created in man a great aspiration, the aspiration for unity with the Divine, the spiritual value of which it is impossible to exaggerate.

### *The Ascending and the Descending Movement: Evolution and Involution*

But nevertheless it is one-sided. It takes into account only one aspect of the world-process—the aspect of ascent. But there is the other aspect of it also—the aspect of descent. In fact, without the descent of the Spirit into the world, there cannot be any ascent of the world into the Spirit. To the extent to which the Spirit has descended into the world, to that very extent is it possible for the world to ascend into the Spirit. There is a descent of the Spirit even into Matter. That is why Matter seeks to evolve into something higher than Matter—Life. There is a descent of the Spirit into Life, and that is why Life seeks to rise to something higher than itself—Mind. Similarly, there is a descent of the Spirit into Mind, and Mind must therefore move towards its Source by ascending to something higher than itself—Supermind. The ascending process does not stop with the Supermind but continues till the Absolute Spirit or Sachchidananda is reached.

The descending process is called Involution, and the ascending process Evolution. Everywhere Evolution is conditioned by Involution. The evolution of Matter is possible only because there has been an involution of the Spirit into Matter. Had there not been a deposit of the Spirit in Matter, the latter could not have evolved. That is why it is so necessary to look upon Matter also as spiritual. That is why the one-sided spiritual view which totally ignores Matter is so fundamentally wrong. You cannot talk of evolution and yet deny the spiritual element in Matter. As with Matter, so is it with Life, Soul and Mind. There can be no talk of any upward movement of these unless each of these bears the stamp of the Spirit upon its back. Ascent without descent, evolution without involution is unthinkable. The Vedantist in his enthusiasm for the ascent of the human consciousness into the Divine forgets this fundamental fact. He ignores altogether the mainspring of all evolution—the descent of the Spirit into the minutest particle of Matter.

Evolution reproduces in the reverse order the process of the descent of the Spirit in involution. The order of involution, as sketched by Sri Aurobindo, (Vide *The Life Divine*, Vol. I, p. 403) is as follows : Existence, Consciousness-Force, Bliss, Supermind, Mind, Psyche (or Soul), Life, Matter. The order of evolution will therefore be : Matter, Life, Psyche, Mind, Supermind, Bliss, Consciousness-Force, Existence. The first four constitute the lower hemisphere, the last four the upper hemisphere. The stages in the lower hemisphere constitute the subordinate forms of those in the upper hemisphere. "Mind is a subordinate power of Supermind which takes its stand in the standpoint of division. Life is similarly a subordinate power of the energy aspect of Sachchidananda, it is Force working out form and the play of conscious energy from the standpoint of division created by Mind; Matter is the form of substance of being which the existence of Sachchidananda assumes when it subjects itself to this phenomenal action of its own consciousness and force" (*Ibid.*, p. 402). Psyche or Soul is similarly a subordinate power of the third divine principle of Infinite Bliss, but a power "in terms of our consciousness and under the conditions of soul-evolution in the world."

The knot between the higher and the lower hemispheres is where Mind and Supermind meet with a veil between them.

"The rending of the veil is the condition of the divine life in humanity; for by that rending, by the illuminating descent of the higher into the nature of the lower being and the forceful ascent of the lower being into the nature of the higher, mind can recover its divine light in the all-comprehending supermind, the soul realize its divine self in the all-possessing, all-blissful Ananda, life repossess its divine power in the play of omnipotent Conscious-Force and matter open to its divine Liberty as a form of the divine Existence" (*Ibid.*, p. 404).

The changes brought about by the descent of Supermind into Mind and the consequent evolution of Mind into Supermind have further been described as follows : "And this means the evolution not only of an untrammelled consciousness, a mind and sense not shut up in the walls of the physical ego or limited to the poor basis of knowledge given by the physical organs of sense, but a life-power liberated more and more from its mortal limitations, a physical life fit for a divine inhabitant and—in the sense not of attachment or of restriction to our present corporeal frame but an exceeding of the law of the physical body,—the conquest of death, an earthly immortality" (*Ibid.*, p. 399).

An earthly immortality ! Here we have, in fact, one of the most startling features of Sri Aurobindo's conception of evolution. Our evolution to a higher state does not mean any severance from our body, life, soul or mind, but it means a complete transformation of these. In their transformed condition many of their characteristics which are merely accidental, that is to say, which belong to them only in their present unregenerate state, will disappear. For instance, death is not an inherent characteristic of life, but is only a feature of it so far as it is subservient to the operation of Mind. Thus, when Life is freed from the operation of Mind, as it will be on the descent of the Supermind, it will not be any longer subject to death.

With the genius of a true philosopher Sri Aurobindo realizes that to fly from Matter would be really to fly from Spirit. If the Spirit is truly to be the supreme principle, there is no escape from the position that Matter must also be spiritual, in spite of its staggering stupidity and iron necessity. To spiritualize Matter must therefore be the task of evolution and not escape from Matter.

In fact, escapism is the last thing which finds favour with Sri Aurobindo. In words that breathe lofty heroism and unshakable faith in the supremacy of the Spirit, he says, "Therefore, the exclusive spiritual seeker is justified from his view-point if, disgusted with the mud of Matter, revolted by the animal grossness of Life or impatient of the self-imprisoned narrowness and downward vision of Mind, he determines to break from it all and return by inaction and silence to the Spirit's immobile liberty. But that is not the sole view-point, nor, because it has been sublimely held or glorified by shining and golden examples, need we consider it the integral and ultimate wisdom. Rather, liberating ourselves from all passion and revolt, let us see what this divine order of the universe means, and, as for this great knot and tangle of Matter denying the Spirit, let us seek to find out and separate its strands so as to loosen it by a solution and not cut through it by a violence" (*Ibid.*, Vol. I, p. 371).

The evolution of the world has so far reached four stages : Matter, Life, Psyche and Mind. But the time has now come, says Sri Aurobindo, when Evolution must take a leap into the next higher stage, namely, Supermind. When this leap is taken, there will be a total transformation of the whole world, as has just been explained.

*Where Philosophy and Yoga Meet*

This will be made possible, this ascent from Mind to Supermind, by the descent of the latter into the former through the rending of the veil which separates them. How, however, is this to be effected ? It will be effected by the Divine Shakti. But even if the Divine Shakti comes forward to rend the veil, the veil will not be rent, the light of the Supermind will not illumine our consciousness, unless there is an intense aspiration on our part for it and an opening out of the whole of our body, life, soul and mind for the purpose of receiving the light. Here is the point where philosophy joins hands with Yoga. What philosophy establishes theoretically as a fundamental necessity, we can only realize practically through Yoga.

The Yoga of Sri Aurobindo has for its object nothing else than this—the preparation of the field, so that when the Supramental light descends, it may find the soil fit to receive it. For it is possible that the Divine may knock at our door, and we in our ignorance and stupidity and crass egotism may not open it. That will be nothing short of a calamity. It is Yoga that enables us to avert such a calamity. It teaches us to open all the doors of our body, life, soul and mind to the new light that is coming from above. "The supramental change," says Sri Aurobindo, "is a thing decreed and inevitable in the evolution of the earth-consciousness; for its upward ascent is not ended and mind is not its last summit. But that the change may arrive, take form and endure, there is needed the call from below with a will to recognize and not deny the Light when it comes, and there is needed the sanction of the Supreme from above" (*The Mother*, pp. 83-84). The actual rending of the veil which separates us from the Divine Light can only be done by the Supreme Being; no human effort has the power to do this. Human effort, however, if properly directed, can prepare human beings to receive the Supermind when it descends.

When the veil is rent and the Supermind descends, human beings are raised to a higher level. But that this consummation may take place, three things are necessary, namely, consciousness, plasticity, and unreserved surrender, the nature of each of which is beautifully described at pp. 75-77 of the book *The Mother*. Lest anybody should think that this means that the whole of the human race should be raised *en bloc* to the supramental level, Sri Aurobindo says very clearly, "It must be conceded at once that there is not the least probability or possibility of the whole human race rising in a block to the supramental level; what is suggested is nothing so revolutionary and astonishing, but only the capacity in the human mentality, when it has reached a certain level or a certain point of stress of the evolutionary impetus, to press towards a higher plane of consciousness and its embodiment in the being" (*The Life Divine*, Vol. II, Part II, p. 837).

## *The 'How' and the 'Why' of the World-Process*

### (*a*) The Pure Existent

I have given above a very brief sketch of the world-process as conceived by Sri Aurobindo. I have now to discuss the question of the 'how' and the 'why' of this process.

The problem of Creation and of the world-process after creation has been in all ages the stumbling-block of all monistic philosophers in the East as well as the West. How can the One become Many, and how can the Many remain Many without infringing the Oneness of the One? This problem has proved perplexing as much to our great Acharyas of the

Vedanta as to Plato and Spinoza. Pluralists, of course, have escaped this difficulty, but they have done so at the cost of truth.

Sri Aurobindo has discussed the question very fully in *The Life Divine*. The Absolute Reality, as he conceives it, is the triune principle Sachchidananda, that is, Existence-Consciousness-Force-Bliss. The Absolute as a Pure Existent is no doubt the fundamental reality, but movement, energy, process is equally a reality. We have to acknowledge therefore two fundamental facts—a fact of Being and a fact of Becoming.

Strictly speaking, the Absolute is neither Being nor Becoming, neither One nor Many, but is beyond both. Stability and movement, unity and multiplicity are, in fact, our mental representations of the Absolute. "World-existence," says Sri Aurobindo, "is the ecstatic dance of Shiva which multiplies the body of the God numberlessly to the view; it leaves that white existence precisely where and what it was, ever is and ever will be; its sole absolute object is the joy of the dancing" (*Ibid.*, Vol. I, p. 119). But as it is impossible for us to conceive the Absolute as beyond stability and movement, beyond unity and multiplicity, "we must accept the double fact, admit both Shiva and Kali and seek to know what is this measureless Movement in Time and Space with regard to that timeless and spaceless pure Existence, one and stable, to which measure and measurelessness are inapplicable."

### (*b*) The Mother

The question now arises : What is the nature of this Force which we have just seen is to be regarded as a fundamental fact ? Is it conscious or unconscious ? Sri Aurobindo shows that it must be regarded as conscious, for the difficulties of either the Sankhya position which treats Prakriti as unconscious or that of the Western materialists who try to derive consciousness from a material force, are really insuperable. But the most formidable obstacle to the acceptance of the fact that Force is conscious is the most widely prevalent view that all consciousness is mental waking consciousness. On account of this view people fail to understand that consciousness is operating in Nature. But this view is absolutely false, so much so that Sri Aurobindo declares that "it must now definitely disappear from philosophical thinking." Our highest forms of consciousness are in the subliminal condition. Indeed, our subliminal consciousness has a depth and a power of action far exceeding that of our waking consciousness. There is again the supraconscient consciousness which is totally ignored by this view.

Force, being thus Conscious Force, the question arises: In what way does it stand to the Pure Existent which is the Ultimate Reality ? If we suppose this Conscious Force to be the ultimate essence of all existence, then the Pure Existent also cannot remain in its pure existence but is compelled to move. But this view will go against the Absoluteness of the Pure Existent, and is therefore untenable. We have to look upon, therefore, this Conscious Force as inherent in the Pure Existent. Force thus inherent in the Pure Existent may be at rest or may be in motion. When it is at rest, it nonetheless exists; indeed, it is the nature of Conscious Force to have this alternative possibility of rest and motion, the first meaning self-concentration and the second, self-diffusion.

This Conscious Force which is inherent in the Pure Existent (Sat) and which is the dynamical principle at the root of all world-process, is called by Sri Aurobindo *The Mother*. Its nature has been very fully described by Sri Aurobindo in his book *The Mother*.

The Mother is the Divine Shakti which is the operative principle of the universe. But she is veiled by her Yogamaya, so long as she works in the lower hemisphere. "In all that is done in the universe, the Divine through his Shakti is behind all action but he is veiled by his Yogamaya and works through the ego of the Jiva in the lower nature" (*The Mother*, p. 10). So also the Bhagavad-Gita says, *nāhaṁ prakāśaḥ sarvasya yogamāyāsamāvṛtaḥ*.

She appears in three forms: transcendent, universal and individual. "Transcendent, the original supreme Shakti, she stands above the worlds and links the creation to the ever unmanifest mystery of the Supreme. Universal, the cosmic Mahashakti, she creates all these beings and contains and enters, supports and conducts all these million processes and forces. Individual, she embodies the power of these vaster ways of her existence, makes them living and near to us and mediates between the human personality and the divine Nature" (*The Mother*, p. 37). She is further characterized as follows : "All is she, for all are parcel and portion of the divine Conscious Force. Nothing can be here or elsewhere but what she decides and the Supreme sanctions; nothing can take shape except what she, moved by the Supreme, perceives and forms after casting it into seed in her creating Ananda" (*Ibid.*, p. 39).

### (*c*) Bliss

I have so far spoken of the 'how' of the world-process. The question of the 'why' remains to be discussed. Why does the Absolute create, and after creating, sustain a world of divers forms ? What is the object that it has in this whole scheme of creation and sustenance of the world ? The answer in one word is : Bliss. It is for the sheer joy of the thing that the Absolute creates and sustains the world. I have already quoted one passage from his book where Sri Aurobindo says, "World-existence is the ecstatic dance of Shiva...its sole absolute object is the joy of the dancing."

The Supreme Reality, Sachchidananda, is not only Existence and Consciousness-Force but also Bliss. Its Absoluteness means also its illimitable bliss of conscious existence. The bliss of Sachchidananda, however, is not confined to the still and motionless possession of its absolute self-being. Just as its Conscious Force projects itself into a world of innumerable forms, so also its self-delight revels in an infinite multiplicity of universes. To enjoy this infinite movement and variation of its self-delight is the object of its creative play of Conscious Force.

Even the relative and the finite can rise above their relativity and finitude in proportion as they share this eternal bliss. Bliss, therefore, is the inherent characteristic of every finite being and of every world-process.

The most formidable obstacle to the acceptance of this view is the presence of evil and of pain and suffering. Unless we are in a position to show that this really is no negation of bliss but is merely a mode of its manifestation, our thesis, namely, that bliss is the inherent characteristic of every finite being and of all world-process, will remain unproved.

Let us meet the difficulty squarely. What is it that is asserted ? In the first place, it is said that the presence of evil is a contradiction of the universality of bliss. Here Sri Aurobindo makes the rather startling assertion that "we do not live in an ethical world." "The attempt of human thought to force an ethical meaning into the whole of Nature is one of those acts of wilful and obstinate self-confusion, one of those pathetic attempts of the human being to read himself, his limited habitual human self into all things and judge them from the standpoint he has personally evolved, which most effectively prevent him from arriving at real knowledge and complete sight" (*Ibid.*, Vol. I, p. 144). This assertion, startling as it is, need not stagger us. For the same assertion has been made by most of the idealistic thinkers of the present day, such as Bradley, Bosanquet and Mackenzie. Their arguments also are very similar to those of Sri Aurobindo. They assert, like Sri Aurobindo, that morality is a peculiar feature of human life and cannot be treated as an ultimate characteristic of reality. In the highest condition morality will lapse into something more complete, something which is a fuller expression of ourselves. Bradley says that morality is an appearance, for it rests upon a fundamental opposition between the ideal that is to be achieved and the actuality that falls far short of it. The highest condition, the ultimate nature of reality is thus 'beyond good and evil.'

Ethics, in other words, is only a stage in evolution. The real factor is the urge of Sachchidananda towards self-expression. "This urge," says Sri Aurobindo, "is at first non-ethical, then infra-ethical in the animal.... And just as all below us is infra-ethical, so there may be that above us whither we shall eventually arrive, which is supra-ethical, has no need of ethics (*Ibid.*, p. 146).

Then, again, with regard to the problem of pain and suffering, it must be remembered that universal bliss is something wider and more comprehensive than what we ordinarily call pleasure, even as universal consciousness is something wider and more comprehensive than our waking consciousness. In its comprehensiveness it embraces both pleasure and pain; in fact, pleasure and pain are only its positive and negative currents. Its first phenomenal manifestations are characterized by the dualism of pleasure and pain, but it rises from these to a supreme delight of being which transcends the distinction of pleasure and pain.

In fact, pleasure, pain and indifference are but the superficial vibrations of our limited self which is uppermost in our waking consciousness. They are an imperfect response of an incomplete self to the multiple contacts of the universe. They are only a prelude to the full and united play of the conscious being in us. They are "not the true and perfect symphony that may be ours if we can once enter into sympathy with the One in all variations and attune urselves to the absolute and universal diapason." "And if we can go back into ourselves and identify ourselves not with our superficial experience, but with that radiant penumbra of the Divine, we can live in that attitude towards the contacts of the world, and standing back in our entire consciousness from the pleasures and pains of the body, vital being and mind, possess them as experiences whose nature being superficial, does not touch or impose itself on our core and real being. In the entirely expressive Sanskrit terms, there is an *ānandamaya* behind the *manomaya*, a vast Bliss-Self behind the limited mental self, and the latter is only a shadowy image and disturbed reflection of the former" (*Ibid.*, p. 158).

Moreover, pleasure, pain and indifference have no absoluteness about them. These reactions of our limited self to the contacts of the universe have only a sanction of habit and no real necessity behind them. We feel pleasure or pain in a particular situation because that is the habit that we have formed. But it is perfectly possible for us to respond in a different way, to feel pleasure when we should have felt pain, and pain when we should have felt pleasure. It is further within our competence to return, instead of the habitual modes of reaction, pleasure, pain and indifference, the response of inalienable delight which is the experience of the true Bliss-Self within us.

Thus the presence of evil and pain in no way contradicts the universal principle of Bliss which is the motive force of the whole universe.

### *Transition to the Supermind*

I have so far dealt with Sri Aurobindo's conception of the nature of the Supreme Reality as a Pure Existent manifesting itself as a Conscious Force and creating out of sheer self-delight. But the creation of a finite world out of the Infinite Conscsiousness requires an intermediate principle, a principle of selective knowledge which alone can fashion finite appearance out of the infinite reality. The difficulties of Spinoza's theory of modes teach us the necessity of such an intermediate selective principle. This intermediate selective principle of knowledge cannot, however, be regarded as Mind, for this will lead to Illusionism or Mayavada, as Mind distorts Reality by arbitrary division. It must, says Sri Aurobindo, be a selective principle of knowledge which retains the real truth of existence. In other words, it must be a Supreme Truth-Consciousness. To this Supreme Truth-Consciousness, the Creator of the world of finite beings, Sri Aurobindo has given the name *Supermind*. It is the link between Sachchidananda and the finite world.

## CHAPTER II

# THE SUPERMIND AND THE PSYCHIC BEING

### *The Supermind*

In the previous chapter we have shown that a link is necessary between Sachchidananda and the world, and that this link cannot be Mind. Mind has certain fundamental limitations which render it unfit to serve as a link between God and the world. "Mind," as Sri Aurobindo points out, "is not a faculty of knowledge nor an instrument of omniscience; it is a faculty for the seeking of knowledge, for expressing as much as it can gain of it in certain forms of a relative thought and for using it towards certain capacities of action." He further says, "It is the power which interprets truth of universal existence for the practical uses of a certain order of things; it is not the power which knows and guides that existence and therefore it cannot be the power which created or manifested it" (*The Life Divine*, Vol. I, pp. 178-79).

It is clear, therefore, that the link must be something higher than Mind. It must retain the true nature of Sachchidananda and not exhibit it in a veiled, distorted or diluted form. It must at the same time be the consummation and fulfilment of Mind and not merely related to it as something transcendent. Such a link is the Supermind.

The Supermind is called by Sri Aurobindo 'Real-Idea'. By giving it this name he wants to emphasize the fact that it is "a power of Conscious Force expressive of real being, born out of real being, and partaking of its nature, and neither a child of the Void nor a weaver of fictions. It is conscious Reality throwing itself into mutable forms of its own imperishable and immutable substance" (*Ibid.*, p. 177).

Sri Aurobindo also calls it a Truth-Consciousness. The name, he says, he has borrowed from the Rig-Veda. In the Rig-Veda 'Rita-cit' means "the consciousness of essential truth of being (*satyam*), of ordered truth of active being (*ṛtam*) and the vast self-awareness (*bṛhat*) in which alone this consciousness is possible."

The Supermind thus is the Creative Idea which retains to the full the truth of the Supreme Reality. Mind, Life and Matter are an inferior expression of it which serves as a goal towards which these are trying to move. It creates a world of "phenomenal reality of variable conscious being which, inevitably drawn towards its own essential Reality, tries at last to recover it entirely whether by a violent leap or normally through the Ideal which put it forth."

It is, in fact, nothing else than God as Lord and Creator. It is, however, different from the Ishvara of the Vedantist or the Demiurge of Plato. The Ishvara of the Vedanta is not the Absolute in its pure untarnished form. It is the Absolute seen through its reflection in Maya, which reflection partially disguises and even distorts its true nature. Sri Aurobindo in this matter wants to go back to the unsystematized Vedanta of the Upanishads, which is innocent of this conception of a Maya-ridden Ishvara, and to the standpoint of the Vedas. The sages who said, "यतो वा इमानि भूतानि जायन्ते। येन जातानि जीवन्ति। यत् प्रयन्त्यभिसंविशन्ति," did not contemplate a Creator who was himself shrouded in Maya.

The Supermind is likewise different from the Demiurge of Plato. The Greek philosophers were in a fix to explain the origin of motion. Parmenides denied motion altogether, and the result was that the whole of creation was nothing but an illusion to him. Anaxagoras, a realist, took the created world to be real, but he had to face the difficulty of accounting for the generation of motion from a plurality of static beings. This difficulty he tried to solve with the help of the principle of Nous or Reason which, being incorporeal, he thought could alone impart motion. But the Nous has no relation whatsoever either to the infinity of primeval seeds or to the world of generation which it helped to bring about. It was a pure *deux ex machina*, brought in for the sake of solving an insoluble difficulty.

The difficulty persists even in Plato. In the account of creation which he gives in the 'Timaeus', Plato conceives the Demiurge or Creator as creating according to an archetype or pattern. But if that be the case, what is his relation to the archetype ? Is the archetype created or not created ? Plato reluctantly declares that it cannot be created, for then it would be imperfect, and God would in that case be creating the world according to an imperfect pattern, which could not be, as it would militate against God's goodness. But if it is not created, then either God would be subordinate to it or it would be co-eternal with God. Jowett in his masterly introduction to this dialogue has tried his best to explain the difficulty, but he has to confess that it does not admit of any satisfactory solution. "We must reply again," he says, "that we cannot follow Plato in all his inconsistencies, but that the gaps of thought are probably more apparent to us than to him. He would perhaps have said that the 'first things are known only to God and to him of men whom God loves'." There are other difficulties in Plato's theory of creation, namely, his admission of a prior existence of Matter and also the problem of Evil, which are traceable to the same cause, namely, the loose manner in which his conception of a Creator is related, on the one hand to the Ideas and on the other, to the world of creation.

Sri Aurobindo's conception of the Supermind is free from the difficulties of the Vedantist or of Plato. Their mistake lay in thinking that the creative principle was something different from the ultimate reality. The result of this was either (as in the case of the Vedanta) that the world came to be regarded as unreal, or (as in the case of Plato) that the unity of the system was destroyed and the Ultimate Principle, the Creator and the World fell asunder.

The only philosopher I can think of who has succeeded in maintaining a continuity between the Absolute Reality, the Creator and the created world is Hegel. But Hegel did this work with the help of his logic and by making Thought all in all, which suffered from the very serious defect that it gave no recognition to Will or to the suprarational powers of cognition.

The conception of the Supermind is the pivot round which the whole of Sri Aurobindo's philosophy moves. It is of the utmost importance to understand its true nature, and I shall therefore have to present in greater detail his view of it. Fortunately for us, Sri Aurobindo has dealt with it very exhaustively in his book *The Life Divine*.

### *Supermind and Mind*

The Supermind is the culmination and consummation of Mind. It is all that the Mind strives to be but cannot attain. Mind by its very nature is a consciousness which cuts up and breaks asunder the forms of things from the indivisible whole in which alone they can really exist. It treats the parts as if they could exist independently. Not that it wants always to remain shut up in the parts. It has a constant urge to go beyond the parts and reach the whole. But unfortunately, all its attempts to do so end in failure, for, as Sri Aurobindo points out, in the very attempt "it falls from its own firm ground into the ocean of the intangible, into the abyss of the infinite, where it can neither perceive, conceive, sense nor deal with its subject for creation and enjoyment." This is the truth which Kant clumsily expressed by saying that when knowledge tries to soar to the region of the Unconditioned or the Absolute, it floats simply in mid-air and loses itself in interminable contradictions. What he should have said was that is was only when mental knowledge tries to do so, that it finds itself confronted with hopeless contradictions. His great mistake was in taking mental knowledge to be the only knowledge accessible to man.

Mental knowledge undoubtedly fails to grasp the nature of the Absolute. There Kant is perfectly right. Mind is constitutionally incapable of grasping a whole. It inevitably reduces every whole to a mere aggregate. Its congenital incapacity to comprehend the whole renders it totally unfit to grasp the Infinite. For this reason Sri Aurobindo says, "Mind cannot possess the Infinite, it can only suffer or be possessed by it; it can only lie blissfully helpless under the luminous shadow of the Real cast down on it from planes of existence beyond its reach" (*The Life Divine*, Vol. I, p. 248).

Bergson also said the same thing about mental knowledge. Mental or intellectual knowledge, according to him, suffers from a fundamental defect. It cannot comprehend anything without analyzing or dissecting it into its elements. But such analysis breaks the simple unity of the whole, which cannot be restored by any desperate attempt on the part of the mind to piece together the dissected elements. For the unity which is arrived at in this way is a mere patchwork; it cannot be a substitute for the true unity which knows no division into elements but exists as an integral whole.

Mind, however, is only a subordinate power of the Supermind which is secretly directing its processes and feels itself the urge to come to higher and higher unities. That is why it is not merely content with analysis, but proceeds, however clumsily, however imperfectly, to synthesize the divided units with a view to arriving at the unity of the whole which it broke asunder when it analyzed it into atomic units. Herein lies the salvation of mind, the possibility of its evolving into something higher. Mind saves itself by becoming more than mind, by transforming itself into the Supermind.

Mind, in fact, is a fall from the Supermind, and mind, therefore, is bound to climb again to that from which it fell. This fall is a necessary condition of involution or creation, the descent of the Spirit into the world. What, however, is the inner necessity which drives the Spirit to descend into the mind ? We shall discuss the question when we come to deal with the nature of the process of descent. For the present, we can only say that this descent is only for the sake of the Spirit coming back to itself. So far as the particular descent from the Supermind to the mind is concerned, it is due to the individualized soul concentrating itself upon itself and ignoring others, forgetting that others are also itself. It is due, as Sri Aurobindo beautifully puts it, to the soul forgetting "that all minds are one Mind taking many standpoints, all lives one Life developing many currents of activity, all body and form one substance of Force and Consciousness concentrating into many apparent stabilities of force and consciousness."

These fundamental deficiencies of the mind are rendered still worse in the case of man by reason of the mind's self-identification with the body. Using constantly the body, especially, the brain and the nervous system , as the vehicle of its own expression, it is too much preoccupied with this physical machinery to realize its own pure condition. This applies, of course, to the surface mind; for deeper down there is the subliminal mind which is free from this preoccupation with the body, and which, therefore, is in a position to give a push to the surface mind which contributes not a little to the growth of the mind and its ultimate transformation into something higher.

### *The Supermind and Intuition*

We thus see that there is a vast gulf between Mind and Supermind, and consequently it is necessary to seek an intermediary between them. Can intuition serve as such an intermediary ? What is the relation between the supramental consciousness and intuition ? As there is a lot of misconception on this point, I think it necessary to make clear Sri Aurobindo's views on it and also show how those views are related to those of one of the most celebrated Western philosophers of the present century—I mean Bergson, whose recent death has created a void in the philosophical world which it is difficult to fill. The question, unfortunately, has been further complicated by the ambiguity of the word 'intuition'.

Sri Aurobindo looks upon intuition as a communication to the mind from above. "Intuition", he says, "brings to man those brilliant messages from the Unknown which are the beginning of his higher knowledge" (*Ibid.*, p. 102). He further calls it "a projection of the characteristic action of these higher grades (that is, higher grades of consciousness) into the mind of Ignorance" (*Ibid.*, p. 418). Its value is very great, for it establishes a connection between Mind and what is above it.

Nevertheless it would be wrong to call it the highest form of consciousness. For in human mind "its action is largely hidden by the interventions of our normal intelligence; a pure intuition is a rare occurrence in our mental activity : "for what we call by the name is usually a point of direct knowledge which is immediately caught and coated over with mental stuff, so that it serves only as an invisible or a very tiny nucleus of a crystallization which is in its mass intellectual or otherwise mental in character" (*Ibid.*, p. 418). Very often "the flash of intuition is quickly replaced or intercepted, before it has a chance of manifesting itself by a rapid imitative mental movement, insight or quick perception or some swift-leaping process of thought which owes its appearance to the stimulus of the coming intuition but obstructs its entry or covers it with a substituted mental suggestion, true or erroneous, but in either case not the authentic movement."

Intuition, thus, being overlaid with mental stuff and its flow being frequently interrupted by imitative mental movement, is not in a position to give us that integral experience which alone reveals the ultimate truth. No wonder, then, that it is followed by Reason, for at the level of mind in which we are, Reason alone can organize and articulate our experience. This is, indeed, what happened in our own country when the intuitive age of the Vedas and the Upanishads was followed by an age of Reason. This is not to be regarded as a retrograde movement, as a downward march, for the lower faculty gets an opportunity of assimilating as much as it can of what the higher has left and thereby transforming itself and preparing itself for the reception of the higher truths.

From this brief sketch of the intuitive process as understood by Sri Aurobindo, it would appear that the reason why he does not regard it as the highest form of consciousness is that it is under the influence and control of mind. Human intuition is always more or less under such influence and control and can therefore never be the same as the pure truth-consciousness or supramental consciousness. If it were possible for us to have an intuition completely free from all mental action, then we could have the ultimate truths revealed through it. In fact, Sri Aurobindo calls such an intuition the supreme intuition.

Let us now see what Bergson thought of intuition. He defined intuition in his *Introduction to Metaphysics* as "a kind of intellectual sympathy by which one places oneself within an object in order to coincide with what is unique in it and consequently inexpressible." In another passage of the same book he called it "an intellectual auscultation." It is thus a direct approach to reality which, in Bergson's opinion, enables us to enter into the heart of it. Any other approach, such as, for instance, the intellectual approach, would not, he thought, take us to the heart of reality but would only make us describe a circle round it. It follows, therefore, that the only way of knowing reality is by way of intuition.

This view of intuition, however, is not free from difficulty, and raises a number of questions. In the first place, we may ask : Do we get this intuition naturally, that is, without our seeking it, or does it require any effort on our part to get it ? If it requires an effort, what is the nature of this effort ? Secondly, are the intuitions of all persons of the same value, or even in the same person, are all the intuitions obtained at different moments of the same value ? If not, by what criterion are the values of the different intuitions to be determined ? Unfortunately, Bergson did not give any satisfactory answer to these questions. But he repeatedly spoke in his *Introduction to Metaphysics* of "the effort of intuition," of "a laborious and even painful effort," of "the active, I might almost say violent, character of metaphysical intuition." These expressions suggest that in Bergson's view intuition does not come naturally to us but has to be obtained by an effort. He has, however, nowhere specified what the nature of this effort is and whether by some training this effort may be increased. But at any rate his recognition that intuition has to be obtained by an effort leaves the door open for the possibility that some men have better intuitions than others, and that even in the same man intuitions of various grades of value occur. As I shall show presently, Bergson does clearly recognize that there are grades of intuition. And if that be the case, it cannot be said that any and every intuition is the full and complete revelation of reality.

Bergson regarded metaphysics, that is, the full and complete knowledge of reality, as integral experience. But in view of the obvious difference in value between one intuition and another which Bergson himself admitted, are we not entitled to say that our ordinary human intuition is incapable of giving us this integral experience, and that it is only the highest type of intuition that can be called integral experience ?

That Bergson did recognize grades of intuition appears clearly from his last book *The two Sources of Morality and Religion.* There in a passage which occurs in his account of the philosophical value of mysticism, he contrasted the ordinary intuition of human beings with the deeper intensifications of it in mystic experience. As the matter is of considerable importance, I quote here his exact words : "But just as there subsisted around animal instinct a fringe of intelligence, so human intelligence preserved a halo of intuition. The latter, in man, had remained fully disinterested and conscious, but it was only *a faint glow* and did not radiate very far. Yet it is from this that the light must come, if ever the inner working of the vital impulse were to be made clear in its significance and in its object. For this intuition was turned inward; and if, in a first intensification, it made us realize the continuity of our inner life, if most of us went no further, a *deeper intensification* might carry it to the roots of our being, and thus to the very principle of life in general. Now is not this precisely the privilege of the mystic soul ?" (The italics in these sentences are mine) (*Two Sources*, etc., p. 214).

The difference between Sri Aurobindo's view of intuition and that of Bergson is therefore not so great as at first sight it appears to be. Both look upon integral experience as revealing the true nature of reality. Both think that human intuition at its present level is not capable of giving this integral experience, and therefore of revealing the true nature of reality. But while Bergson put all the different strata of consciousness, from integral experience to the ordinary human intuition, under the same title 'intuition', Sri Aurobindo has made a more thorough-going analysis of them and has differentiated the different layers, giving them different names. He has also very clearly shown why it is that human intuition falls short of integral experience. Bergson, although he has based the whole of his philosophy upon intuition, has unfortunately not indicated, in a manner free from ambiguity, the nature of intuition and has not also shown on what principle the gradation of intuition can be made.

### *Supermind and Overmind*

In our search for a link between Mind and Supermind, we came across Intuition. Intuition no doubt is a revelation to us of a truth which is not ordinarily accessible to the mind. But, as we have seen, it is too flashy, too unstable, too much under the influence of masses of mental stuff that penetrate into it, to be able really to serve as a link between Mind and Supermind. It itself has its source in something higher, "a superconscient cosmic Mind in direct contact with the Supramental Truth-Consciousness." This superconscient cosmic Mind is the link between Mind and Supermind, and is called by Sri Aurobindo the Overmind. His description of it in

*The Life Divine* is a wonderful piece of literary art : it combines the richest poetic imagery with the highest flights of philosophical thought. We are told, for instance, that it "covers as with the wide wings of some creative Oversoul this whole lower hemisphere of Knowledge-Ignorance, links it with that greater Truth-Consciousness, while yet at the same time with its brilliant golden Lid it veils the face of the greater Truth from our sight, intervening with its flood of infinite possibilities as at once an obstacle and a passage in our seeking of the spiritual law of our existence, its highest aim, its secret Reality" (*Ibid.*, Vol. I, p. 424).

Although the Supermind communicates all its realities to the Overmind, yet the latter is "a first parent of the Ignorance," because it lacks the integrality of the Supermind. It takes each aspect or power of the Supreme Reality and constitutes it into a separate and independent reality. Thus the integrality of the supramental consciousness, in which all the different aspects or powers of Reality exist harmoniously in one whole, is destroyed in the Overmind. "Purusha and Prakriti, Conscious Soul and executive Force of Nature, are in the supramental harmony a two-aspected single truth, being and dynamis of the Reality; there can be no disequilibrium or predominance of one over the other. In Overmind we have the origin of the cleavage, the trenchant distinction made by the philosophy of the Sankhyas in which they appear as two independent entities, Prakriti able to dominate Purusha and cloud its freedom and power, reducing it to a witness and recipient of her forms and actions, Purusha able to return to its separate existence and abide in a free self-sovereignty by rejection of her original overclouding material principle. So with the other aspects or powers of the Divine Reality, One and Many, Divine Personality and Divine Impersonality, and the rest" (*Ibid.*, p. 426).

Employing the ideology of the Vedas, Sri Aurobindo says, "If we regard the Powers of the Reality as so many Godheads, we can say that the Overmind releases a million Godheads into action, each empowered to create its own world, each world capable of relation, communication and interplay with the others." And just as in the Vedas each god is worshipped as if he were himself the Supreme God, although each is a separate deity, acting sometimes in opposition to the other deities, sometimes in harmony with them, so the Overmind erects each of the powers of the Supreme Reality into a separate reality, with its separate action and principle of development, although it shows also how it combines harmoniously with the other powers of the Supreme Reality.

Further, he says, "Overmind consciousness is global in its cognition and can hold any number of seemingly fundamental differences together in a reconciling vision" (*Ibid.*, pp. 428-29). Where the mind sees irreconcilable differences, the Overmind intelligence perceives coexistent correlatives; what to the mind are contraries are to the Overmind complementaries.

### *Psychic Being or Chaitya Purusha*

We have so far dealt with the surface consciousness—the surface mind, life and matter. But there is also an inner substratum within us. There is a subliminal mind, life and matter which is more plastic, more powerful, more capable of dynamic action than our surface mind, life or body. Bend the surface mind, which is all that is brought outwardly to our view, there is "a subliminal mind which is not hampered by our actual mental life and its strict limitations, something large, powerful and luminous, the true mental being beind that superficial form of mental personality which we mistake for ourselves."

So also we have two lives, one outer, involved in the physical body, bound by its past involution in Matter, which lives and will also die, and the other, "a subliminal force of life which is not cabined between the narrow boundaries of our physical birth and death, but is our true vital being behind the form of living which we ignorantly take for our real existence." Similarly, we have a double body, for behind our visible body, there is "a subtler material existence which provides the substance not only of our physical but also of our vital and mental sheaths."

So, too, we have a double soul. We have the surface soul or the desire-soul which works in our vital cravings and emotions and our efforts to seek power, knowledge and happiness, and our inner soul, our true psychic being or *caitya puruṣa*, "a pure power of light, love, joy and refined essence of being."

The soul or psyche is not life or mind or matter, but is, as Sri Aurobindo expresses it, "the opening and flowering of the essence of all these to their own peculiar delight of self, to light, to love, to joy and beauty and to a refined purity of being." It is that term of our being through which the divine principle of Bliss acts in us, as the divine principle of Supermind operates through Mind and the divine principle of Pure Existence manifests through Matter.

Leaving aside the desire-soul, which stands in the way of our realizing our true soul-life, we have the psychic being or the *caitya puruṣa* which is the central core of our being. Sri Aurobindo lays the greatest stress upon the awakening of this psychic being or our true soul. "The malady of the world," he says, "is that the individual cannot find his real soul" (*The Life Divine*, Vol. I, p. 338). To find our real soul is the first step towards the attainment of our true spiritual life.

The nature of this psychic being Sri Aurobindo has explained very fully in his *Lights on Yoga*. There he has divided the central being of man into two layers. The upper, which he calls the Jivatman, is a spark of Divinity, a portion of the Divine Self (Paramatman); it is a transcendent principle which is above the manifestation in individul life and presides over it. The lower, which is the psychic being, is the immanent principle, the deputy of Jivatman, which stands behind the manifestation in individual life and supports it. If the Jivatman is called a Divine spark, then the psychic being is this spark growing into a fire, for its function is to kindle the spark into a flame, shedding its light over the whole of our being. Sri Aurobindo calls it also a Child, the Son of God (*Lights on Yoga*, p. 31), because it bears on its face the stamp of its divine origin.

In *The Life Divine* (Vol. I., p. 344) he further characterizes it as "a flame born out of the Divine and, luminous inhabitant of the Ignorance, grows in it till it is able to turn it towards the Knowledge. It is the concealed Witness and Control, the hidden Guide, the Daemon of Socrates, the inner light or inner voice of the mystic. It is that which endures and is imperishable in us from birth to birth, untouched by death, decay or corruption, an indestructible spark of the Divine." It is, as the Upanishads describe it, the Purusha seated within the heart, no bigger than the thumb:

अङ्गुष्ठमात्रः पुरुषोऽन्तरात्मा सदा जनानां हृदये संनिविष्टः ।।

Sri Aurobindo, however, warns us against a possible misconception. Although this psychic being is indispensable to our spiritual progress, we must not think that it alone can open to us all the gates of the Spirit. These gates will only open to us when the light from the Supermind descends upon us. In no other way is it possible for us to reach the higher levels of the Spirit. Sri Aurobindo is very definite on this point. "But it might seem, then," he says, "that by bringing this psychic entity, this true soul in us, into the front and giving it there the lead and rule, we shall gain all the fulfilment of our natural being that we can seek for and open also the gates of the kingdom of the Spirit. And it might well be reasoned that there is no need for any intervention of a superior Truth-Consciousness or principle of Supermind to help us to attain to the divine status or the divine perfection. Yet, although the psychic transformation is one necessary condition of the total transformation of our existence, it is not all that is needed for the largest spiritual change". (*The Life Divine*, Vol. I., p. 347). The same thing he has also said in Vol. II, Part II, pp. 939 *et seq.* of the same book.

CHAPTER III

# THE DESCENT OR INVOLUTION

## *The Plunge into Ignorance*

So far our discussion has been about the nature of the Creative Principle. We have now to deal with the process of Creation. Creation is a plunge of the Spirit into Ignorance. Why, however, should it be necessary for the Spirit to descend into Ignorance for the sake of creation ? Why can it not create out of the fulness of its self-consciousness ? The Spirit can create, and does indeed create, out of its plenary self-consciousness, remaining throughout perfectly in knowledge. Such creation, in fact, is creation in the upper hemisphere, and represents the crown and apex of the whole creation. Our sages were aware of such a pure creation through complete self-manifestation and called it the greater world beyond the lesser, but they regarded the world in which we men live as a mixed world of light and darkness, of truth and error. The creation of this latter world can only be through Ignorrance; it cannot be through knowledge. But although it is a plunge into Ignorance, it is a plunge for the purpose of coming back again through the whole gamut of creation to light and knowledge. That is the meaning of the world-process : to come back to light after an initial plunge into darkness or the sea of Inconscience. Immortality and peace and harmony are not given in this world but have to be built up out of death and struggle and discord. The plunge is, indeed, for the sake of giving the world an opportunity of rising out of ignorance and suffering and weakness into knowledge and bliss and strength. The diving into Ignorance is only for the sake of bringing up on the surface by slow but sure stages the rich treasures of the Superconscient. It is to give man, apparently a hopelessly frail creature, the very picture of helplessness and misery, the seemingly hopeless task of rising to immortality, knowledge and strength.

Creation, therefore, of the world in which we live, is the result of the plunge of the Spirit into Ignorance, but in spite of this plunge, or rather because of it, the created world carries with it the promise of the millennium, the assurance that out of its present hopelessly weak and miserable state it will emerge into one of perfect strength and bliss. It is the realization of this which, as Sri Aurobindo points out, has taken different shapes in different ages —"the perfectibility of man, the perfectibility of society, the Alwar's vision of the descent of Vishnu and the gods upon earth, the city of God, the millennium, the new heaven and earth of the Apocalypse." It is this which has been through all ages the source of inspiration for all noble efforts and great achievements of man.

### *The True Nature of Ignorance*

But the question that now arises is : What is Ignorance ? It is not enough to say that the Absolute plunges into Ignorance for the sake of creation. What we have a right to ask is : What is the nature of this Ignorance ? How does Ignorance arise at all ? The answer to this question Sri Aurobindo has given in his own inimitable way in the chapter "The Knowledge and the Ignorance" in the first part of the second volume of *The Life Divine.*

Sri Aurobindo shows that if we look upon Knowledge and Ignorance as fundamentally opposed to each other, as the Vedanta, when it crystallized itself in the systems of the great

Acharyas, took them to be, then even if we regard Ignorance as a power of Brahman, there would result no unitary conception of Reality, but rather Reality would be divided hopelessly at its source, and we should have to take shelter under the plea that the ultimate nature of Ignorance is an unfathomable mystery. Escape from this position is only possible if we take Ignorance itself to be Knowledge, no matter how partial and fragmentary and distorted it may be, and further, if we view Ignorance itself to be capable of evolving into Knowledge. What we require is to realize that Consciousness or Knowledge operates in three different ways. At the highest it is Divine Self-Knowledge, which is also Divine All-Knowledge. At the other extreme we have what seems to be a complete negation of knowledge, an "effective dynamic, creative Nescience." In the intermediate process we call it Ignorance, which is a sort of half-way house between the Supreme Consciousness and the complete Nescience.

Ignorance, indeed, is nothing else than the power of the Divine Consciousness to partially withhold itself, to check or regulate itself. It is not, then, in any sense a separate Power or separate Will existing by the side of, and independently of, the Divine Power.

It is also capable, without self-annulment, of evolving itself into knowledge. Knowledge is the natural culmination of Ignorance, not a violent change which it undergoes by a complete self-effacement. "In fact," as Sri Aurobindo puts it, "what is happening is that the Ignorance is seeking and preparing to transform itself by a progressive illumination of its darkness into the knowledge that is already contained within it; the cosmic truth manifested in its real essence and figure would by that transformation reveal itself as essence and figure of the supreme omnipresent Reality" (*Ibid.*, Vol. II, Part I, p. 312).

## *Origin of Ignorance*

We have not yet discussed the question of the origin of Ignorance, althogh we have seen the importance of this question, for all processes in the lower hemisphere are processes through Ignorance. This problem will have to be discussed from the point of view of an integral Oneness as the ultimate truth. The problem, in fact, as Sri Aurobindo puts it, is this : "How could this manifold ignorance or this narrowly self-limiting and separative knowledge arise and come into action or maintain itself in an absolute Being who must be absolute consciousness and therefore cannot be subject to ignorance ? How is even an apparent division effectively operated and kept in continuance in the indivisible ?" (*Ibid.* pp. 413-14).

It will not do, he points out, to say either that Ignorance is cosmic, as some schools of the Vedanta assert, or that it is individual, as some other schools affirm. For in either case, it will destroy the integral Oneness of the Supreme Consciousness. Still less is it open to assert a fundamental difference between the Jivatman and Brahman, taking the former to be subject to Ignorance and the latter to be totally free from it. We have therefore to say, if we are to maintain the integral oneness of the Supreme Reality, that "Ignorance must be part of the movement of the One, a development of its consciousness knowingly adopted, to which it is not forcibly subjected but which it uses for its cosmic purpose" (*Ibid.* p. 415).

But this also does not remove the whole difficulty. How can Ignorance be a part of a movement of knowledge, and what is the cosmic purpose for which Ignorance is employed ?

To answer this question, we have to observe that the Absolute is not merely Chit or Consciousness but also Shakti or Power. Chit itself is also Shakti. We may call it Tapas, using the word in the Vedic sense of a conscious force acting upon itself or upon its object—the sense, for instance, in which the Vedas say that the world was created out of Tapas. If we examine our own consciousness, we find that this Tapas, or the energy of the conscious force applying itself to an object, is really the most essential dynamic force that we possess. But in us this dynamism can only work upon two objects, namely, ourselves, that is, the internal world, and others, whether creatures or things, that is, the external world. But in the Absolute reality the operation of this dynamism will be somewhat different. For there is no distinction there between the inner and the outer, between Self and Not-Self. Moreover, in us only a part of our dynamism is manifested in our voluntary action, the rest being to our mental consciousness either involuntary or subconscious or superconscious, but in the Absolute Reality it is not so, for all is its own indivisible self and all actions are movements of its own indivisible will. Tapas, therefore, for the Supreme Being, "is the integral Tapas of an integral consciousness in an indivisible Existence" (*Ibid.* p. 421).

Now when we further examine our own consciousness, we find that there is an active part of it as well as a passive part of it. But even in the passive part of our consciousness, if we open ourselves sufficiently to what is beyond, we feel the presence of a Power acting upon us, a Power which is transcendental and which works in us for a greater manifestation of knowledge. Thus we see the energizing of Tapas both in what we call our active and our passive consciousness.

It is the same with the Absolute. Both its active and its passive consciousness are Tapas. Its active consciousness is that part of it which melts into creation. But that does not represent the whole of its being. The unmelted part of its being is the great reservoir from which proceed its further acts of creation. We realize this very clearly in our own consciousness. Thus, when we act, there is the whole of our personality standing behind the act. But not the whole of it expresses itself in the action. Only a small fragment of it does so, the rest remaining as a source of potential power, capable of projecting itself at any moment into action. There is therefore a vast gap between the expressed part of our being, which constitutes active consciousness, and the infinitely greater part which is what we call the passive consciousness. The former is a tiny fragment of the latter, an infinitesimal part of the vast treasure-house of unspent energy, which is the unexpressed part of our being.

The passive consciousness of Brahman and its active consciousness are, therefore, not two different things; "they are the same consciousness, the same energy, at one end in a state of self-reservation, at the other cast into a motion of self-giving and self-deploying, like the stillness of a reservoir and the coursing of the channels which flow from it" (*Ibid.*, p. 425). There is thus not a passive Brahman and an active Brahman, but one Brahman, one Reality which we call passive when it reserves its Tapas and active when its Tapas expresses itself in action, in creation.

We should further note that the activity and passivity of Brahman do not alternate each other, as they do in human consciousness; for if they did, then while creation continued, there would be no passive Brahman in existence, all would be action, and when the universe was dissolved, there would be no active Brahman, everything would lapse into eternal lifeless immobility. For Brahman, therefore, both the active and the passive consciousness exist simultaneously.

The Bhagavad-Gita says: "यस्मात् क्षरमतीतोऽहमक्षरादपि

चोत्तमः" The Supreme Reality transcends both the mobile and the immobile parts of its being. It is aware of both and is not lost in either. Ignorance, therefore, is not a power of the Supreme Being nor does it dwell in Him. Consequently, there cannot be any primeval Ignorance.

But neither is it an inherent characteristic of the multiplicity of souls. For if it were so, none of these souls could ever aspire to rise above Ignorance and come into the presence of Knowledge. It is only when the individual soul is in the superficial layer of consciousness that it is shut out from the larger consciousness which would show its unity with other souls and with the Supreme Being. But it has also open to it the deeper levels of consciousness where the individual soul sees itself in fundamental unity with other souls and with the whole universe.

The origin of Ignorance must therefore be sought elsewhere. It must be sought, says Sri Aurobindo, "in some self-absorbed concentration of Tapas, of Conscious-Force in action on a separate movement of the Force; to us this takes the appearance of mind identifying itself with the separate movement and identifying itself separately with each of the forms resulting from it" (*Ibid.*, p. 435). The result of this self-absorption of Tapas is "that it builds a wall of separation which shuts out the consciousness in each form from awareness of its own total self, of other embodied consciousnesses and of universal being."

But what is the nature of this self-absorption, this self-forgetful concentration ? It cannot be the action of the whole being or the whole force of being, for the character of that action is whole knowledge. It must therefore be a partial movement absorbed in a superficial or partial action of consciousness which makes it oblivious of everything that is not included in its formation. Ignorance, therefore, says Sri Aurobindo, "is Nature's purposeful oblivion of the Self and the All, leaving them aside, putting them behind herself in order to do solely what she has to do in some outer play of existence" (*Ibid.*, p. 438).

Man by nature is not ignorant. He has the power and potency in him of complete knowledge. It is only because for pragmatic reasons, for purposes of the superficial movements of his life, he lives absorbed in the present moment, that there is erected a wall which shuts him out completely from all knowledge of the future and also from all knowledge of the past, except for that small part of it which memory makes accessible to him. His existence for the moment is not the whole truth of his being, but only a pragmatic truth which holds good for the limited purposes of his superficial life.

Ignorance, therefore, does not create any dualism. It is not something opposed to knowledge, not something which contradicts knowledge. It is a power of knowledge itself, "a power of Knowledge to limit itself, to concentrate itself on the work in hand, an exclusive concentration in practice which does not prevent the full existence and working of the whole conscious being behind, but a working in the conditions chosen and self-imposed on the nature.... This power of self-limitation for a particular working, instead of being incompatible with the absolute conscious-force of that Being, is precisely one of the powers we should expect to exist among the manifold energies of the Infinite" (*Ibid.*, p. 457).

One cannot help being reminded here of a similar attempt made by Bergson to show that the two movements of Reality, one directed towards life, freedom, the other directed towards matter, necessity, are really not two movements but essentially one. But Bergson's critics point out[1] that he has not been

[1] See M'Kellar Stewart's *A Critical Exposition of Bergson's Philosophy*, p. 117.

able to effect a real union between the two for he has not succeeded in showing why the free creative activity of the Spirit should reverse its current and move towards Matter. There is nothing in the nature of the Spirit, as conceived by Bergson, which warrants such a reversal of movement.

Here one sees the superiority of Sri Aurobindo's position. By conceiving the ultimate Reality as Consciousness-Force and by showing the need for the self-limitation of this Force for purposes of creation, Sri Aurobindo has been able to get rid of a difficulty which has proved such a stumbling-block in the system of Bergson.

### *Special Form of Descent of the Spirit : Avatara*

We have so far discussed the ordinary form of descent of the Spirit, the descent through Ignorance, which is responsible for the creation, as well as the maintenance of the world-process. But the world-process sometimes requires a special form of descent of the Spirit. This is the descent as Avatara which is mentioned in the Bhagavad-Gita. The peculiarity of this descent is that it is a descent in human form of the whole of the Divine Personality. In the fourth chapter of the Gita the nature of this special descent as Avatara and the reason for it have been very clearly stated. The Gita clearly shows (*The Gita,* iv. 6) that there is no contradiction in the idea of God taking birth in a human form. On the contrary, it says that no knowledge of God is complete unless there is the knowledge of this kind of Divine birth (iv. 9). Sri Aurobindo has discussed this question of Avatara very fully in his *Essays on the Gita,* a summary of which I have given elsewhere (Vide my article in the *Uttara,* Bhadra 1347). As this chapter has already become very lengthy, it is not possible for me to do more than merely state the most salient points in Sri Aurobindo's conception of Avatara. In the first place, Sri Aurobindo says that the upholding of Dharma is not the only object of the descent of the Avatara, for it is not in itself an all-sufficient object, but is only "the general condition of a higher aim and a more supreme and divine utility." "For," he says, "there are two aspects of the divine birth; one is a descent, the birth of God in humanity, the Godhead manifesting itself in the human form and nature, the eternal Avatar; the other is an ascent, the birth of man into the Godhead, man rising into the divine nature and consciousness, *madbhāvam āgatāḥ*; it is the being born anew in a second birth of the soul. It is that new birth which Avatarhood and the upholding of the Dharma are intended to serve" (*Essays on the Gita*, First Series, p. 216). He continues : "If there were not this rising of man into the Godhead to be helped by the descent of God into humanity, Avatarhood for the sake of the Dharma would be an otiose phenomenon, since mere Right, mere justice or standards of virtue can always be upheld by the divine omnipotence through its ordinary means, by great men or great movements, by the life and work of sages and kings and religious teachers, without any actual incarnation. The Avatar comes as the manifestation of the divine nature in the human nature, the apocalypse of its Christhood, Krishnahood, Buddhahood, in order that the human nature may by moulding its principle, thought, feeling, action, being on the lines of that Christhood, Krishnahood, Buddhahood transfigure itself into the Divine" (*Ibid.*, p. 217).

For Sri Aurobindo, therefore, the main significance of the conception of Avatara is the birth of man into the Godhead, as he very beautifully puts it, and not merely the preservation of Dharma. The Avatara is born, in his view, in order to show man what he is capable of becoming. It is to give him an ocular demonstration that he can also become God without even leaving his body. Otherwise he thinks there is no necessity for Avatarhood, the ordinary way in which God reveals Himself being quite sufficient for the ordinary processes of the world. "The Divine," says Sri Aurobindo, "works behind indeed and governs its special manifestation through this outer and imperfect consciousness and will, but is itself secret in the cavern, *guhāyām*, as the Veda puts it, or as the Gita expresses it, 'In the heart of all existences the Lord abides turning all existences as if mounted on a machine by Maya.' This secret working of the Lord hidden in the heart from the egoistic nature-consciousness through which he works, is God's universal method with creatures. Why then should we suppose that in any form he comes forward into the frontal, the phenomenal consciousness for a more direct and consciously divine action? Obviously if at all, then to break the veil between himself and humanity which man limited in his own nature could never lift" (*Ibid.* p. 225).

This is also what the Gita itself says. Thus Sri Aurobindo points out, "That the Gita contains as its kernel this second and real object of the Avatarhood, is evident from this passage—"अवजानन्ति मां मूढा मानुषीं तनुमाश्रितम् । परं भावमजानन्तो मम भूतमहेश्वरम् ॥" (ix-11)—by itself rightly considered; but it becomes much clearer if we take it, not by itself—always the wrong way to deal with the texts of the Gita—but in its right close connection with other passages and with its whole teaching" (*Ibid.* p. 218).

## CHAPTER IV

# THE ASCENT OR EVOLUTION

### *The General Nature of the Evolutionary Process*

The process of evolution, as we have already seen, is made possible by the process of involution. It is because of the descent of the Spirit into Matter, Life and Mind, that these can ascend to the higher regions of the Spirit. In fact, evolution is nothing else than "a heightening of the force of consciousness in the manifest being so that it may be raised into the greater intensity of what is still unmanifest, from matter into life, from life into mind, from the mind into the spirit."

This process of evolution is a triple one, which we may call a widening, a heightening and an integration. First of all, it means a widening of the field, providing greater room for the operation of each principle as it emerges, secondly, it means an ascent from grade to grade, from the lower to the higher, and thirdly, it means taking up within itself, as soon as it reaches a higher grade, all the previous lower grades and transforming them, so that at each step of the ascent, there is not merely an ascent to a higher principle but a lifting up and transformation of all the lower grades. Integration thus implies a descent of the higher principle into all the lower ones; in fact, it is ascent through descent. Thus when the principle of mind evolves, there is not merely the emergence of this new principle but a descent of it into all the lower ones, leading to an uplifting and transformation of matter and life, so that life and matter become different after the emergence of mind from what they were before its emergence. This is a very important thing which we must bear in mind in understanding

Sri Aurobindo's conception of evolution, and here we see a vital difference between his view of evolution and all other views of evolution, both Eastern and Western. There is no Eastern or Western philosopher who has stressed this very essential feature of evolution, as Sri Aurobindo has done. The usual view of evolution, which looks upon it as a mere ascent from the lower grade to the higher grade, may be compared to the march of an army which advances without keeping its lines of communication with the base intact. And we may compare Sri Aurobindo's conception of evolution with the march of an army which advances with the whole force, keeping all its lines of communication perfectly intact. An evolution, which is merely the isolated lifting of a part of the nature of a being by dissociating it from the other parts, is of as little significance from the evolutionary point of view, as the isolated landing of some advanced troops into enemy territory, which is effected without any attempt to maintain the lines of communication with the main army, is from the military point of view. This is the reason, Sri Aurobindo explains, why although many sages, both in our country and in other lands, have obtained individual salvation by detaching themselves from the rest of the world, there has been no general uplift of the whole world, no transformation of it into a higher status of being. This clearly shows that if we are to attain that supreme condition of being which we are destined sooner or later—sooner, as Sri Aurobindo believes, rather than later—to attain, the means to it must be different from that in which mankind has so long believed, namely, detaching oneself from one's body, life and mind and landing, by means of an ecstatic trance, individually into a divine sphere.

As a result of this triple process of evolution there is a rapid change of the basis of inconscience into a basis of complete consciousness, a complete change of the action of ignorance into the action of knowledge. This change is, of course, only partial in us and is completed only in what we call the superconscient. Each ascent brings with it a partial change and transformation of the old nature taken up and subjected to a new principle. Thus, inconscience will be turned into a partial consciousness, into an ignorance desperately striving for knowledge. But at some point of the ascent, knowledge, that is, a true consciousness or the consciousness of the Spirit, must be substituted for the inconscience and the ignorance.

The starting-point of evolution is Inconscience : its middle point is Ignorance, and its final goal is Knowledge. An evolutionary process must by its very nature be a development in some first established principle of being. This first basic principle is Matter. Evolution first takes place in Matter. Mind and Life are evolved in Matter. This puts a certain limitation upcn them, the limitation to use the substance of Matter for their operation and also the limitation of being subject to the law of Matter, even while they go on modifying its substance. For they do modify the substance of Matter, first into the substance of life and then into conscious substance. But they do not succeed in transforming it altogether; they cannot make it completely alive and perfectly conscious. When life first evolves in Matter, it is bound to death; so also when mind first evolves, it is matter-bound and life-bound. This clearly shows that neither Mind nor Life is the original creative Energy; they, like Matter, are only intermediaries. This original Energy, therefore, we must seek for in something higher than Life or Mind, in some deeper Reality which has not yet revealed itself in our universe.

Since neither Matter nor Life nor Mind is the original

creative Power, it is clear that this Power must be some Consciousness higher than life-consciousness or mind-consciousness, an energy more potent than material energy. Since it is higher than mind, it must be supramental Consciousness-Force; as, moreover, it is a power more potent than material energy, it must be a power of the Spirit. Neither material energy nor life-force or mind-force can effect a total transformation of material substance; if, therefore, such a transformation is to take place, it can only be by the full emergence of the Spirit. This emergence will mean a conversion of the inconscient in us into the conscient, spiritualizing our material substance, planting the law of the gnostic consciousness in the whole of our being and finally changing the mental into a supramental being. This is the culminating stage of evolution; more correctly, it is that stage which first decisively changes the character of evolution by transforming its character of Ignorance and its basis of Inconscience into a movement of Knowledge.

So much for Cosmic Evolution. But evolution is also individual. It may be said to have, like the god Siva, a triple eye, an eye turned upwards, an eye turned downwards, and an eye turned inwards. We have so far spoken of its upward eye and its downward eye, its ascent and its integration. But it has also an eye turned inwards, that is, towards that small thing, no bigger than a man's thumb, as the Kathopanishad calls it, which is our Soul. Evolution is as much individual as it is cosmic. The recognition of this great truth is another original feature of Sri Aurobindo's conception of evolution. "The immense importance of the individual being," he says, "which increases as he rises in the scale, is the most remarkable and significant fact of a universe which started without consciousness and without individuality in an undifferentiated Nescience. This importance can only be justified if the Self as individual is no less real than the Self as Cosmic Being or Spirit and both are powers of the Eternal" (*The Life Divine*, Vol. II, Part II, p. 704).

The individual is not a mere accompaniment or auxiliary product of the play of consciousness in the body but is a persistent reality, an eternal portion of the Eternal Spirit. He is the medium through which the Spirit discloses its being. Behind all the changes of our personality and upholding them, there is a Person, a real spiritual Individual, a true Purusha. This Purusha is nothing else than the Supreme Spirit dwelling within us. The discovery of this Purusha dwelling within us is an essential condition of the discovery of the Cosmic Self and the Supreme Reality.

The individual Purusha, in working out his cosmic relations with the Supreme Spirit, has to assume a body; it is this which is his starting-point for the expression of himself in this universe. This assumption of body is what we call birth; through it only is it possible to have a progressive development of our conscious being towards unity with God and with all in God. Birth, therefore, is an essential condition of the manifestation of the Purusha on the physical plane. But this birth, whether in the human form or in any other, cannot be an isolated phenomenon without a past which was preparatory to it or a future for its further fulfilment. Birth, therefore, of any individual soul in a body must be continued in other births and must have been preceded by other births. Any other view, any view, for example, which would treat the birth of the soul in an individual human body as an isolated phenomenon without any relation either to a previous birth of the soul in some other body or a subsequent birth of it, would be extremely illogical. There is a rhythm in the individual evolution as there is a rhythm in the cosmic evolution. The progressive evolution of the Spirit in the

Cosmos has its counterpart in the progressive evolution of the individual soul through different births. If rebirth were not a fact, then the evolution of the soul would also cease to be a fact. In fact, as Sri Aurobindo puts it, "re-birth is self-evidently a necessary part, the sole possible machinery of such an evolution. It is as necessary as birth itself; for without it birth would be an initial step without a sequel, the starting of a journey without its further steps and arrival. It is re-birth that gives to the birth of an incomplete being in a body its promise of completeness and its spiritual significance" (*The Life Divine*, Vol II, Part II, p. 718).

The question of re-birth also raises the interesting question whether the soul immediately after death takes birth in the the physical plane or whether it rests for some time in some supra-physical plane before taking birth again in this physical plane, for the possibility of the existence of such planes cannot be ruled out on *a priori* grounds. This question has been discussed very fully by Sri Aurobindo in the chapters *The Order of the Worlds* and *Re-birth and other Worlds* in *The Life Divine*, Vol. II, Part II.

We thus see that evolution means a transformation of the whole of our terrestrial existence, material, mental and vital, first by an ascent to a higher principle, and secondly, by a psychicization, as we may call it, of the whole being, that is to say, a transformation of the whole being through the light emanating from the Soul. The first transformation, again, consists of two stages : (1) the transformation by ascent to the higher reaches of the mind, and (2) the transformation by ascent to the Supermind and the descent of the latter. Thus, evolution means a triple transformation. We shall now briefly explain the nature of this triple transformation.

## *Triple Transformation*

This triple transformation is thus indicated by Sri Aurobindo : "There must first be the psychic change, the conversion of our whole present nature into a soul-instrumentation; on that or along with that, there must be the spiritual change, the descent of a higher Light, Knowledge, Power, Force, Bliss, Purity into the whole being, even into the darkness of our subconscience; last, there must supervene the supramental transmutation,—there must take place as the crowning movement the ascent into the supermind and the transforming descent of the supramental consciousness into our entire being and nature" (*Ibid*, p. 911).

The first step in this transformation is the psychic change. We have already stated in our second chapter the main features of Sri Aurobindo's conception of the soul. The soul or psyche is the inner or hidden part of our nature, although it is by virtue of it that we exist and continue as individual beings. While the other parts of our being change and perish, the psychic entity is immutable and imperishable. It is not tarnished by the impurities of our surface being, but "is an ever-pure flame of the divinity in things, and nothing that comes to it, nothing that enters into our experience can pollute its purity or extinguish the flame." It is the permanent being in us which employs mind, life and body as its instruments but itself remains unaffected by their operations.

The first step in the needed transformation is to remove the veil which hides this inner being and let its light flood the whole of our surface being, life, mind and matter. We do get even in our normal mental life glimpses of this inner being of ours, for we do have a certain sensitive feeling for what is true and good and beautiful, fine and pure and noble.

Indeed, we say that a man who has not got this sensitive feeling has no soul. We do recognize this as a diviner part of our true nature. This is all true, but this is not enough. What is wanted is a full development of this psychic being, so that it may lead to a transformation of mind, life and matter.

Our psychic being or soul-personality is not born in us, like Minerva, fully armed. It evolves slowly and is at first very weak and indistinct. Its strength depends upon the power of the soul that has succeeded in asserting itself on our surface consciousness against the opposition of Inconscience and Ignorance. As there is greater emergence of the soul in Nature, there is a further development of our psychic being, an increase in its communion with the soul behind and an improvement in its communication to the mind and life and body on the surface. But its development will be very slow if it is left entirely to its own unaided action. It can only be rapid when man feels a need to bring the soul to the front and allow it to master his life and mind and body. This is the first essential for a psychic transformation of our being : we must be educated to feel the need of the growth of our psychic being and the sovereignty of the soul over the rest of our being. How this education is to be effected, how the psychic personality is to be developed has been very thoroughly explained by Sri Aurobindo in his *The Life Divine*, Vol. II, Part II, pp. 918-33 and also in his *Lights on Yoga*. It is indeed a vital part of his Yoga, for without a full development of our psychic personality, the purpose of the Yoga, which is to make us fit to receive the light from the Supermind when it knocks at our door, will be frustrated.

But the awakening of the soul in us and the development of our psychic being will not alone lead to that total transformation of our terrestrial existence, which is the purpose of Evolution. For unless there is a descent of the higher realms of the spirit, the flowering of our psychic being will take place only within the limited sphere of the regions of mind, life and matter in which we dwell. Therefore, the opening of the soul should take place along with the opening out outwards of mind, life and matter to the higher light of the spirit. It is no doubt true that the psychic transformation very greatly facilitates the ascent to the higher spiritual life, but it can never be a substitute for the latter. Thus the second transformation we require is the transformation by the spiritual consciousness. As Sri Aurobindo puts it, "the psychic movement inward to the inner being, the Self or Divinity within us, must be completed by an opening upward to a supreme spiritual status or a higher existence."

When the ascent to the higher reaches of consciousness takes place without a corresponding descent of the latter, then there is no permanent transformation of being. There is only a vision of an infinity above us, of an infinity of consciousness, force and bliss, of a boundless light, a boundless power and a boundless ecstasy. But such a vision fades away gradually after return to the previous level; some remembrance of it may remain, but it ceases to be a dynamic force; the lower consciousness falls away from it, and there is no permanent transformation of our being. Even if such ascent takes place frequently and is made at will, there is nothing more than a partial retention in consciousness of the impressions of a temporary sojourn in the higher spiritual planes.

But if there is a descent of the higher consciousness, of the higher intuition and the overmental consciousness, then the effects of the ascent will become permanent. There will be a permanent raising of the level of our being. As a result of this, matter, life and mind will become very different from what they are at present. Indeed, we shall become altogether different beings, much nobler and purer than we are to-day. For, as Sri Aurobindo puts it, this descent "brings to us the abiding spiritual sense and awareness of the infinite and eternal with a great largeness of the nature and a breaking down of its limitations; immortality becomes no longer a belief or an experience but a normal self-awareness; the close presence of the Divine Being, his rule of the world and of our self and natural members, his force working in us and everywhere, the peace of the infinite, the joy of the infinite are now concrete and constant in the being; in all sights and forms one sees the Eternal, the Reality, in all sounds one hears it, in all touches feels it; there is nothing else but its forms and personalities and manifestations; the joy or adoration of the heart, the embrace of all existence, the unity of the spirit are abiding realities" (*Ibid*, p. 946).

But the spiritual change we have sketched above will not lead to man's attaining the highest spiritual level of which he is capable, unless there supervenes the third and final transformation. This is the transformation by the supermind which completes the passage of the soul through ignorance and for the first time places its consciousness, its life and power upon a completely effective basis of self-knowledge.

## *Ascent to the Supermind*

The final stage of evolution, or rather that stage which first causes a radical change in the whole of terrestrial existence, physical, vital and mental (for above the Supermind there are the still higher stages, Bliss, Consciousness-Force and Pure Being), is the supramental change, due to the ascent to the Supermind made possible by a descent of the latter.

The supramental change is something so radically different from what we can conceive with our mental consciousness that a description of it is impossible with the help of our language, which can only express what is accessible to our mind. The only redeeming feature is that the supramental consciousness is already at work in the whole of the evolutionary process; it is indeed a supreme development of elements which are at work already in us, though in a rudimentary and diminished form.

The transition to Supermind is really a passage from Nature to Supernature. This being so, it is not in the power of mind to effect this transition. All the previous stages of evolution that we have described are stages in ignorance, but the supramental change is a stage in knowledge. There is no supramental being or organized supermind nature acting either on our surface consciousness or in the depths of our normal subliminal consciousness. Consequently, the emergence of the Supermind is not possible unless there is a direct descent of it.

No doubt we can conceive that as a result of a long process of evolution, our terrestrial nature may come in contact with the superconscient spheres and give rise to an overmental formation, in consequence of which there may emerge a superior race of mental beings who think and act not by reasoning but by an intuitive understanding. This may be followed by an overmentalization which would carry us to the borderland beyond which lies the region of the Supermind. But the process will be an extremely slow one, and will moreover be extremely uncertain. There is also the possibility that what is thus achieved after a long and tiresome process of evolution may be only an imperfect superior mentalization.

Thus the descent of the Supermind into our earthly nature is the only way in which the ascent of the evolutionary process to the Supermind can take place. But there are certain preliminary conditions which must be fulfilled if the supramental descent is to take place. "For a real transformation," says Sri Aurobindo, "there must be a direct and unveiled intervention from above; there would be necessary too a total submission and surrender of the lower consciousness, a cessation of its insistence, a will in it for its separate law of action to be completely annulled by transformation and lose all rights over our being" (*Ibid*, p. 959). In his book *The Mother* he has explained very clearly the nature of the surrender without which the supramental descent cannot take place. As we have already explained in the opening chapter of this *Introduction*, this does not mean that we can by our efforts force the Supermind to descend; it only means that if our field is not ready for the reception of the supramental light, it may withdraw after descending, and it is for this reason that a complete surrender of our mind, life and body to this higher light is necessary. In fact, the whole of the processes we have described above, the gradual psychicization of our being and the slow spiritualization of our nature by the light of the higher reaches of the mind and the Overmind, are preliminary conditions for the descent of the Supermind.

As a result of the descent of the Supermind, there will be "a real participation by the individual in the working of the universal Consciousness-Force; the individual Purusha would be the master of his own executive energy, and at the same time a conscious partner, agent, instrument of the Cosmic Spirit in the working of the universal Energy; the universal Energy would work through him, but he also would work through her, and the harmony of the intuitive truth would make the double working a single action" (*The Life Divine*, Vol. II, Part II, p. 962).

The greatest difficulty arises in effecting the surrender of

Nature. But without this surrender of Nature, leading to its transformation into Supernature, the ascent to the Supermind is not possible, for what is required is not merely the participation and consent of the Purusha to the supramental change, but also that of Nature. Hence the ascent is very difficult, for it has to contend at every step with mechanized instincts and fixed habits—habits of mind, life, character, whose roots go very deep and which can therefore be rooted out by digging very deep. The task is rendered much easier if there is a proper psychicization of our being, for this effects a tremendous change in all parts of our being.

The order of ascent from Mind to Supermind is as follows : Mind, Higher Mind, Illumined Mind, Intuition, Overmind and Supermind. The nature of each of these has been very fully explained by Sri Aurobindo in *The Life Divine*, Vol. II, Part II, pp. 983 *et seq.*

Although the evolutionary process has to climb so many stairs, yet it need not take a very long time, for with the emergence of the higher levels of mind, the pace of the process will be considerably quickened. The evolution of Matter takes several aeons, that of life progresses much more quickly, that of mind much more quickly still, while when spiritual evolution begins, a vast increase in the rapidity of the pace becomes possible.

The final stage is the descent of the Supermind. When this takes place, Nature becomes transformed into Supernature and human beings into Gnostic Beings.

CHAPTER V

# THE GNOSTIC BEING AND THE DIVINE LIFE

## *The Gnostic Being*

When the Supermind will descend, there will take place a radical transformation of all existence, material, vital and mental. Evolution does not, of course, stop with the emergence of the Supermind, for above the Supermind there are the still higher principles of Bliss, Consciousness-Force and Pure Being, but when the Supermind emerges, there is a radical change in the character of evolution, for henceforth it will be through knowledge and not through ignorance. As a result of this radical change human beings will be transformed into gnostic beings or beings who have shed all ignorance and are illumined by the light of knowledge. This does not however mean, as we have explained at the outset, that the whole human race will become a race of gnostic beings.

One thing we must make quite clear, namely, that any attempt to convey the nature of the supramental being by means of language, which means the description of it in terms of mental categories, must from its very nature be doomed to failure, for there is a vast gulf between the nature of Supermind and that of Mind. "At the same time," as Sri Aurobindo puts it, "certain deductions can be made from the very fact of this difference of nature which might be valid at least for a general description of the passage from Overmind to Supermind or might vaguely construct for us an idea of the first status of the evolutionary supramental existence." Readers of Bradley's *Appearance and Reality* will be reminded of a similar statement made by Bradley, that although philosophy should be in a position to give a general outline of the nature of the Absolute, yet a detailed description of it was impossible.

Throughout the course of evolution through Inconscience and Ignorance there has been a division between the surface self and consciousness and the subliminal self and consciousness, the surface self being formed under the influence of the push from below of the Inconscient slowly developing a concealed force of the spirit, the subliminal, partly in this way, but mainly by the influence of the force coming from above. Before the descent of the Supermind can take place, this division must disappear, for the supramental light will descend upon the entire consciousness. With the emergence of the Supermind the rule of the Inconscient will vanish, for it will be converted into (what it no doubt has been all along in reality) Superconscience, and as a result of this, there will be the first formation of a gnostic consciousness and nature.

The supramental descent will affect the nature of the lower evolutionary stages also; something of its light and its force will penetrate downwards and awaken the lower regions to a greater action of the hidden truth in them. A dominant principle of harmony will descend upon the life of Ignorance; "the discord, the blind seeking, the clash of struggle, the abnormal vicissitudes of exaggeration and depression and unsteady balance of the unseeing forces at work in their mixture and conflict, would feel the influence and yield place to a more orderly pace and harmonic steps of the development of being, a more revealing arrangement of progressing life and consciousness, a better life-order" (*The Life Divine*, Vol. II, Part II, p. 1031). There will also emerge in human life a freer play of intuition and greater sympathy and understanding. In place of a constant and confused struggle between the forces of light and the forces of darkness, there will arise a gradual progression from lesser light to greater light.

Will the race of supramental or gnostic beings be all of one type ? Sri Aurobindo answers : No. "A supramental or gnostic race of beings would not be a race made according to a single type, moulded in a single fixed pattern; for the law of the supermind is unity fulfilled in diversity and therefore, there would be an infinite diversity in the manifestation of the gnostic consciousness, although that consciousness would still be one in its basis, in its constitution, in its all-revealing and all-uniting order" (*Ibid.* p. 1034).

The gnostic individual will be the consummation of the spiritual man : his whole being will be governed by the power of a vast universal spirituality. "All beings would be to him his own selves, all ways and powers of consciousness would be felt as the ways and powers of his own universality." He would be in the world and of the world, but also would exceed it in his consciousness : "he would be universal but free in the universe, individual but not limited by a separative individuality."

How would the supramental being act ? "He would act," says Sri Aurobindo, "in a universal awareness and a harmony of his individual self with the total self, of his individual will with the total will, of his individual action with the total action." He would not feel the difficulty which we feel, of harmonizing ourselves with other selves and with the world, for he has no ego. It is our ego which acts as a barrier between ourselves and our fellows; it is this which erects barriers of self-interest, completely shutting us off from others. With the disappearance of the ego, these walls separating us from others would also disappear. For really there is no conflict between the individual and the universe. Both are simultaneous and interdependent expressions of the same Supreme Reality. There must be a right relation between the two, and but for our ego we should have discovered it. The supramental being possesses this right relation as his right and privilege.

His experience of the universe will be that of one living in the universe, but at the same time that of one who carries the universe with him. "He will have the cosmic consciousness, sense, feeling, by which all objective life will become part of his subjective existence and by which he will realize, perceive, feel, see, hear the Divine in all forms; all forms and movements will be realized, sensed, seen, heard, felt, as if taking place within his own vast self of being."

The gnostic being can have "no aim of being except to be, no aim of consciousness except to be conscious of being, no aim of delight of being other than its delight." He has no desires, no wants, nothing to strive for or achieve. All that we, groping in ignorance, blindly seek to achieve, he fulfils in knowledge. For him all knowledge is self-knowledge of being, all action the self-force of being, and all delight a universal delight of self-existence. For him there cannot be any discovery of the unknown, but only a bringing out of the known. Everything for him is only "the finding of the self by the self in the self."

His relation with the body is also of a totally different kind from that of ours. In us the body is the instrument of the action of the soul. But the body, even in obeying, limits the soul's action; it has, moreover, a law of its own action which the soul cannot fully control. But in the gnostic being the will of the spirit directly controls the movements and the law of the body. He has, working in him, the dynamic spiritual force of the Truth-Consciousness, and this acts in him as a sovereign Reality. It is this which in him rules the action of the body, turning it into a true and proper instrument of the Spirit.

This new relation between the soul and the body enables

the Supermind to accept the whole of material nature, instead of rejecting it. Our rejection of it is due to our failure to control it. But in the Supermind there cannot be any question of such a failure. Thus, the gnostic being's acceptance of material nature is due to a "changed communion of the Spirit with Matter, a control, a reversal of the present balance of interaction which allows physical Nature to veil the Spirit and affirm her own dominance. In the light of a larger knowledge Matter also can be seen to be the Brahman, a self-energy put forth by the Brahman, a form and substance of Brahman."

One more question concerning the gnostic being we must mention before we pass on to our author's conception of the Divine Life. Do pain and suffering exist for him ? If not, how are they transformed ? In asking this question, we have to point out that spiritual ascent brings with it a tranquillity and a power to view with equanimity all pleasures and pains, and that this can pass from the mind to the vital parts and establish there too a similar endurance and apathy; this state may form itself even in the body. At a still higher level, at the level of the Overmind, there comes into existence a power to change the vibrations of pain into those of Ananda. This fact clearly indicates the possibility of a complete reversal of the ordinary rule of the reacting consciousness, and we can therefore understand how the supramental change must bring about the completeness of this reversal. The Divine principle of Ananda is inherent in the gnostic consciousness as a universal delight and transforms everything sordid and miserable into an expression of Ananda.

## *The Divine Life*

We have now to ask : What is our ultimate destiny ? What is the final goal towards which human life is moving ? In other words, what is the character of the Divine Life ?

The Divine Life is already working out in Time; it already exists in us as a necessity and a potentiality, it is the secret reality of our being. Upon it rests the possibility of our fulfilling our destiny.

For our destiny is not to be confined eternally to our present life : it is to exceed the present life and evolve into the higher life, the Divine Life, which is secretly working within us. Our present life is manifestly unfinished. As mental beings, we have an imperfect life, because mind is a very inadequate expression of the consciousness of Being. Even if mind were perfected, there would still remain a great deal to be realized, for the Power that is working within us is not a mind but a spirit, and mind is not the proper dynamism of the consciousness of the spirit but the supermind.

It is difficult to say where the mental life ends and the divine life begins, for they project into each other. There is a good deal of intervening space where they overlap. This interspace is where we can see the process of the higher life in the making. As more of the light of the spirit illumines the mind and life, they put on something of the divinity, and this goes on increasing until the interspace is crossed and the whole existence is unified by the light and power of the spiritual principle. But something more is needed. "This illumination and change must take up and re-create the whole being, mind, life and body : it must be not only an inner experience of the Divinity, but a remoulding of both the inner and outer existence by its power." Not only this, but "it must take form not only in the life of the individual but as a collective life of gnostic beings established as a highest power and form of the becoming of the Spirit in the earth-nature."

But our life is not merely the outer life which is visible to us, but the inner life which is not dependent upon any outer manifestation of external being. This inner life has a supreme significance; the outer has a value only in so far as it expresses the inner nature. The Bhagavadgita says that the true *yogin*, whatever may be his outer life, has an inner life, "dwells in Me" ("सर्वथा वर्तपानोऽपि स योगि मयि वर्तते" vi. 31). This inner life is really what constitutes the true life of a man.

This is, however, only one aspect of the truth, and not the whole truth. However important it may be for an individual to realize his inner life, it is not the only thing which matters. For, as our author points out (*Vide The Life Divine*, Vol. II, Part II, pp. 1107-8), "from the point of view of a spiritual evolution, this would be only an individual liberation and perfection in an unchanged environmental existence : for a greater dynamic change... of the whole principle and intrumentation of life and action, the appearance of a new order of beings and a new earth-life must be envisaged in our idea of the total consummation, the divine issue."

Here the supramental change becomes a matter of paramount importance; a radical change in the character of the physical Nature and of terrestrial existence becomes a fundamental necessity. For what is wanted is the emergence of a divine life on earth, not the isolated realization by a few individuals of their true inner life.

At the same time the whole foundation of the divine life must be inward and not outward. It is the spirit, the inner Reality, that has built up and employs the mind, life and body as its instruments; these latter are merely means and do not exist for themselves. Although in our present life of Nature, it seems as if the world creates us; in reality, it is we who create ourselves and our world. Thus it is the inner life which is of essential importance, everything else being merely its expression and result. Although we are outwardly thrown into a world which is material, ignorant, imperfect, and feel ourselves absolutely helpless in the midst of such a mute, inconscient obscurity, "yet we are vaguely aware of something that is there in us or seeking to be, something other than what has been made, a spirit self-existent, self-determining, pushing the nature towards the creation of an image of its own occult perfection or Idea of perfection."

Our first preoccupation, therefore, if we are really to grow into a divine life must be our inner life. Our next preoccupation is to convert our whole surface being, our thought, feeling and action in the world into a perfect instrument of that inner life. Only if we live in this inner life can we generate a force for creating a better world, for, as our author emphatically declares, "a perfected human world cannot be created by men or composed of men who are themselves imperfect."

Another very important truth he states here. "Knowledge, thought, action," he asserts, "whether religious, ethical, political, social, economic, utilitarian or hedonistic, whether a mental, vital or physical form or construction of existence, —cannot be the essence or object of life" (*Ibid.*, p. 1113). He continues: "To become ourselves is the one thing to be done; but the true ourself is that which is within us, and to exceed our outer self of body, life and mind is the condition for this highest being, which is our true and divine being, to become self-revealed and active."

A divine life must therefore be first and foremost an inner life; there can be no divinity in the outer expression if there is no divinization of the inner being. The divinity in man dwells veiled within him; there cannot be any higher existence for man unless there is in him the reality of an eternal self and spirit.

"To be and to be fully is Nature's aim in us." But to be fully means, in the first place, to be wholly conscious of one's being. Unconsciousness, half-consciousness can have therefore no place here. Secondly, to be fully is to have the integral and intrinsic force of one's being. Thirdly, to be fully means to have the full delight of being. Lastly, to be fully means to be universally, and that means to be transcendentally. It excludes therefore all limited existence in a small restricted ego. It excludes also all dependence on body or embodied mind or embodied life or dependence on this condition or that condition of being or this world or that world.

To live an inner life does not mean imprisonment within the four walls of one's personal self; on the contrary, it is the first step towards a true universality. It brings to us the truth of ourselves as well as the truth of other selves, for this inner living can penetrate the life of all much more thoroughly than any surface consciousness can do. It is for this reason that in the gnostic or divine being, in the gnostic or divine life, there is a complete and intimate knowledge of the self of others, a complete and intimate knowledge of their mind, life, physical being. This enables the gnostic being to act not out of a mere surface sentiment of love and sympathy, but out of this full and intimate knowledge of other selves.

The mental method of mechanization and standardization is just the reverse of this method of inner living. In the life of gnostic communities there will be no attempt made to secure artificial uniformity. There will be perfect tolerance of diversity among different gnostic communities; each will create its own body of the life of the spirit. There will also be allowed free diversity in the self-expression of individuals in the same gnostic community, for this diversity can never create any chaos or discord, because a single consciousness-force, of which all are aware, and of which all feel themselves to be instruments, will harmonize all their actions.

Harmony is the natural rule of the spirit; it is a spontaneous consequence of unity in diversity. In a pure and blank unity there is no place for harmony; nor is there any room for it in utter and absolute diversity. In a gnostic unity in multiplicity the harmony would be there as a spontaneous expression of the unity, which presupposes a mutuality of consciousness and an awareness of other consciousness by a direct inner contact and interchange. In human life harmony is achieved through sense-knowledge and mental perception and communication of ideas by language, but these means are imperfect, and consequently, the harmony achieved is also incomplete. In a gnostic life, a life of superreason and supernature, harmony is achieved through a self-aware spirituality of being and a spiritual interchange of nature. And this harmony is much more perfect and enduring than that achieved by mental means.

In mystic experience there are often engendered new powers of consciousness which are not found in our ordinary mental life. Such powers every seeker after spiritual salvation is asked to discard, for the possession of such powers has the tendency to create in their possessor an ego-consciousness which is fatal to spiritual progress. But when new powers emerge as an inevitable result of the growth into a greater consciousness and a greater life, and this growth is part of the very aim of the spiritual being within us, then this ban has no meaning, for they are a natural, normal and spontaneous product of the new higher consciousness into which the being enters in the course of his self-evolution.

We have briefly sketched above the nature of man's evolutionary destiny. Let us, in the light of this, take stock of our present position in the evolutionary progression. We have in our longing for a personal perfection and the perfection of the life of the race the elements of our future evolution clearly present, but they are present in a rather confused and discordant manner, due to our half-enlightened knowledge. There is a clash between the different ideas—the ideas of individual perfectibility and the full development of the collective being in society. This leads to exclusive emphasis being sometimes laid on the individual and sometimes on society. In the one view the individual is the centre of the whole system; society is there only as a field of activity and growth of the individual man. In the other, the collective life is the only thing that counts, the individual exists only for society, he has no use or purpose save as an instrument of society. In this way human thought has been divided into two mutually hostile camps, called respectively, individualism and socialism, and the human mind with its limitations is not in a position to effect any reconciliation between the rival claims of these hostile camps.

This represents an evolutionary crisis through which mankind is passing. This crisis itself is a part of a more general crisis which Sri Aurobindo describes as follows :

"At present mankind is undergoing an evolutionary crisis in which is concealed a choice of its destiny; for a stage has been reached in which the human mind has achieved in certain directions an enormous development, while in others it stands arrested and bewildered and can no longer find its way. A structure of the external life has been raised up by man's ever-active mind and life-will, a structure of an unmanageable hugeness and complexity, for the service of his mental, vital, physical claims and urges, a complex political, social, administrative, economic, cultural machinery, an organized collective means for his intellectual, sensational, aesthetic and material satisfaction. Man has created a system of civilization which has become too big for his limited mental capacity and understanding and his still more limited spiritual and moral capacity to utilize and manage, a too dangerous servant of his blundering ego and its appetites. For no greater seeing mind, no intuitive soul of knowledge has yet come to his surface of consciousness which could make this basic fullness of life a condition for the free growth of something that exceeded it....At the same time Science has put at his disposal many potencies of the universal Force and has made the life of humanity materially one; but what uses this universal Force is a little human individual or communal ego with nothing universal in its light of knowledge or its movements, no inner sense or power which would create in this physical drawing together of the human world a true life unity, a mental unity or a spiritual oneness" (*The Life Divine*, Vol. II, Part II, pp. 1159-61).

What is the solution of this crisis ? Well, the solution is that given in the last chapter of *The Life Divine*. Live your true inner life, for that is the first step towards the divine life. That will be the best way to create a life of unity, mutuality and harmony.

# CONCLUSION

We have tried to give some of the main ideas of Sri Aurobindo's philosophy. The account is necessarily meagre, for his philosophy, in its gigantic sweep and colossal range, covering the whole realm of mind, life, matter, and laying bare the hidden truths of the soul and the higher regions of the spirit which are at best but dimly felt by us, has perhaps no equal in breadth and comprehensiveness of outlook in the whole range of the history of philosophy. The only philosophers who can be compared with him in this respect are Plato and Hegel in the Western world and Sankara in our land. But in one respect, his outlook is even more comprehensive than that of these philosophers, for he envisages a world in which Spirit and Matter, Life and Mind are all essential ingredients and work harmoniously together, and where truth is achieved not by a negation or annulment of any of these, but by a transformation and transmutation of them in the light of the Highest. Here Hegel perhaps comes nearer to him than any other philosopher either in the West or in the East. For it was he who laid before us the secret of the onward march of the Absolute Idea through the realms of Nature and History, treating these not as negations to be annulled or oppositions to be conquered, but as progressive stages in the evolution of the Absolute in Time. But even Hegel did not envisage the possibility of the Absolute shedding the full glory of its light upon these nether regions. For the Absolute only works, according to him, unconsciously in Nature and consciously, but not self-consciously in History. Evolution must therefore go beyond Nature and History before the Absolute can reach the final stage of its progression in time. There can thus be no possibility of man continuing his life in Nature and having his relations with his fellowmen and yet receiving the supreme blessing from the Absolute Spirit which will convert him into a Divine man.

In Sri Aurobindo's philosophy for the first time man and his terrestrial life have received their full recognition. He is the first to declare that it is possible for man in this terrestrial life, in this physical body, to attain complete Divinity. Divinity is not something which man can only win by getting out of his mind, life and body, but remaining in the physical universe, continuing to dwell in the body and having intercourse with his fellow-men, it is possible for him to become a Divine man. Not only possible, but it is certain that he will become, sooner or later, sooner rather than later, a Divine man.

Here there is a wide divergence between Sri Aurobindo's philosophy and the great Advaita philosophy of Sankara and his school. That philosophy believed man's salvation to lie in his cutting off all ties with the body, mind and life, and becoming merged in the Absolute. This would mean that salvation, if it came, would come only to the individual man; there would be no transformation of the nature of man into that of the Superman or the Divine Man, nor the uplift of the whole universe, physical, vital and mental. But it is precisely this transformation of man into a Divine man, the emergence of a race of Gnostic Beings, representing the culmination and fulfilment of human beings, which is the chief message of Sri Aurobindo's philosophy. And further, he asserts that this transformation of man, this emergence of a race of Supermen will take place in this world, in this terrestrial existence of ours. This terrestrial life will receive the benefit of the higher light that evolution will bring in its train; there will be a general uplift of all the different spheres of existence, physical, vital and mental.

This fundamental difference he has indicated as follows : "The fundamental difference is in the teaching that there is a dynamic divine Truth (the Supermind) and that into the present world of Ignorance that Truth can descend, create a new Truth-Consciousness and divinize Life. The old Yogas go straight from mind into the absolute Divine, regard all dynamic existence as Ignorance, Illusion or Lila; when you enter the static and immutable Divine Truth, they say, you pass out of cosmic existence" (*The Riddle of this World*, p. 69). But although his teaching differs fundamentally from the most well-organized body of philosophical thought in our country, yet it is in complete accord with the spirit of our ancient Scriptures, the Vedas and the Upanishads. For these Scriptures had great faith in the destiny of man and his terrestrial existence, which the later philosophers unfortunately lost. Sri Aurobindo may therefore be said to have revived the ancient teaching of our Vedas and Upanishads concerning the dignity of earthly existence and the high destiny of man.

In his theory of evolution also he makes a fundamental departure from the traditional views of evolution in the East as well as in the West. The traditional view is—and here the East does not differ from the West—that evolution is an ascent from one grade to another, till the highest grade is reached. Sri Aurobindo has shown that if evolution means only this, then it cannot lead to an uplift of the whole being. One part of our being will then have the benefit of the higher light that evolution brings with it, the other parts remaining where they are. If mind receives the new light, then mind alone will rise to a higher state, leaving life and matter precisely where they are. This will not lead to a transformation of our being, but rather to a disintegration of our being, the part which receives light being separated from the other parts. But if evolution means not only ascent but also integration, then an ascent to a higher stage will mean an uplift of all the lower stages. Thus there will be a change of the whole being, the new principle sending its light to the remotest corners of our being.

There is another great truth which Sri Aurobindo has inculcated. Evolution does not mean merely the raising of our surface parts, our surface mind, life and body, but it means also the development of our inner life. Within each of us dwells a spark of Divinity which we call the soul. Evolution requires that the light from the soul should illumine our inner being and through it our outer being. No development of our being is possible without an awakening of our inner being. The movement of evolution therefore, is threefold—one upwards, an ascent, one downwards, an integration, and one inwards, towards the soul.

Such are some of the leading thoughts of Sri Aurobindo's philosophy as we gather them from his *magnum opus*, *The Life Divine*. Slightly changing the memorable words which Max Muller used in connection with Kant's *Critique of Pure Reason*, we may say that if the bridge of thoughts and sighs which spans the history of Aryan culture, as it has evolved so far, has its first arch in the Veda, it has its last in Sri Aurobindo's *The Life Divine*.

## References in Text Updated in Accordance with Sri Aurobindo Birth Centenary Library and its Facsimile Editions

| Text Reference | SABCL Reference |
| --- | --- |
| *Essays on the Gita* | *Essays on the Gita* |
| Series I (1937 Ed.) | Volume 13 (1970 Ed.) |
| *The Life Divine* | *The Life Divine* |
| Volume I (1939 Ed.) | Volume 18 (1970 Ed.) |
| Volume II, Part I (1940 Ed.) | Volume 18 (1970 Ed.) |
| Volume II, Part II (1940 Ed.) | Volume 19 (1970 Ed.) |
| *Lights on Yoga* | *Letters on Yoga* |
| (1935 Ed.) | Volume 22 (1970 Ed.) |
| *The Mother* | *The Mother* |
| (1940 Ed.) | Volume 25 (1972 Ed.) |
| *The Riddle of This World* | *Letters on Yoga* |
| (1933 Ed.) | Volume 22 (1970 Ed.) |

| Text Page | Text Reference | SABCL Reference |
| --- | --- | --- |
| 1 | *LD* I, p. 8 | 18: 17 |
| 4 | *Ibid.*, p. 403 | 18: 264 |
| 4 | *Ibid.*, p. 402 | 18: 263 |
| 5 | *Ibid.*, p. 404 | 18: 264-65 |
| 5 | *Ibid.*, p. 399 | 18: 261 |
| 6 | *Ibid.*, p. 371 | 18: 242-43 |
| 7 | *The Mother*, pp. 83-84 | 25: 40 |
| 8 | *Ibid.*, pp. 75-77 | 25: 36-38 |
| 8 | *LD* II, II,p. 837 | 19: 842 |
| 9 | *LD* I, p. 119 | 18: 78 |
| 11 | *The Mother*, p.10 | 25: 6 |
| 11 | *Ibid.*, p. 37 | 25: 20 |
| 11 | *Ibid.*, p. 39 | 25: 21 |
| 13 | *LD* I, p. 144 | 18: 96 |
| 13 | *Ibid.*, p. 146 | 18: 97 |
| 14 | *Ibid.*, p. 158 | 18: 104-05 |
| 16 | *Ibid.*, pp.178-79 | 18: 118 |
| 17 | *Ibid.*, p. 177 | 18: 117 |
| 20 | *Ibid.*, p. 248 | 18: 163 |
| 22 | *Ibid.*, p. 102 | 18: 67 |
| 22 | *Ibid.*, p. 418 | 18: 274 |
| 23 | *Ibid.*, p. 418 | 18: 274 |
| 27 | *Ibid.*, p. 424 | 18: 278 |

| Text Page | Text Reference | SABCL Reference |
|---|---|---|
| 27 | *Ibid.*, p. 426 | 18: 279 |
| 28 | *Ibid.*, pp. 428-29 | 18: 281 |
| 29 | *Ibid.*, p. 338 | 18: 221 |
| 30 | *Lights*, p. 31 | 22: 265 |
| 30 | *LD* I, p. 344 | 18: 225 |
| 31 | *Ibid.*, p. 347 | 18: 227 |
| 31 | *LD* II,II, pp.939 *et seq.* | 19: 909 *et seq.* |
| 34 | *LD.*,II,I, p.312 | 18: 499-500 |
| 35 | *Ibid.*, pp. 413-14 | 18: 566 |
| 35 | *Ibid.*, p. 415 | 18: 567 |
| 36 | *Ibid.*, p. 421 | 18: 571 |
| 37 | *Ibid.*, p. 425 | 18: 573 |
| 38 | *Ibid.*, p. 435 | 18: 580 |
| 39 | *Ibid.*, p. 438 | 18: 582 |
| 39 | *Ibid.*, p. 457 | 18: 594-95 |
| 41 | *Essays* I, p. 216 | 13: 140 |
| 41 | *Ibid.*, p. 217 | 13: 140 |
| 42 | *Ibid.*, p. 225 | 13: 145 |
| 42 | *Ibid.*, p. 218 | 13: 141 |
| 47 | *LD* II, II, p. 704 | 19: 755 |
| 48 | *Ibid.*, p. 718 | 19: 764 |
| 49 | *Ibid.*, p. 911 | 19: 891 |
| 50 | *Ibid.*, pp. 918-33 | 19: 895-905 |
| 52 | *Ibid.*, p. 946 | 19: 913-14 |
| 54 | *Ibid.*, p. 959 | 19: 922 |
| 54 | *Ibid.*, p. 962 | 19: 924 |
| 55 | *Ibid.*, pp. 983 *et seq.* | 19: 938 *et seq.* |
| 57 | *Ibid.*, p. 1031 | 19: 969 |
| 58 | *Ibid.*, p. 1034 | 19: 971 |
| 62 | *Ibid.*, pp.1107-08 | 19: 1019 |
| 63 | *Ibid.*, p. 1113 | 19: 1022 |
| 67 | *Ibid.*, pp.1159-61 | 19: 1053-54 |
| 70 | *The Riddle*, p.69 | 22: 103-04 |